ALASKA GEOGRAPHIC.

Volume 18, Number 2

Alaska's Volcanoes

The Alaska Geographic Society—

To teach many to better know and more wisely use our natural resources

EDITOR
Penny Rennick

ASSOCIATE EDITOR/PRODUCTION COORDINATOR
Kathy Doogan

STAFF WRITER
L.J. Campbell

DIRECTOR OF SALES AND PROMOTION
Kaci Cronkhite

MEMBERSHIP/CIRCULATION ASSISTANT
Jan Westfall

ALASKA GEOGRAPHIC® (ISSN 0361-1353) is published quarterly by The Alaska Geographic Society, 137 East 7th Ave., Anchorage, AK 99501. Second-class postage paid at Anchorage, Alaska, and additional mailing offices. Printed in U.S.A. Copyright © 1991 by The Alaska Geographic Society. All rights reserved. Registered trademark: Alaska Geographic, ISSN 0361-1353; Key title Alaska Geographic.

POSTMASTER: Send address changes to
ALASKA GEOGRAPHIC®
P.O. Box 93370
Anchorage, Alaska 99509-3370

COVER: This eruption plume spews forth from the summit of Augustine Volcano on March 31, 1986. At its height, the eruptive column reached more than seven miles into the sky above Cook Inlet. *(U.S. Geological Survey)*

PREVIOUS PAGE: Kasilof resident Robert Clucas was on the roof of his house with his camera when Redoubt Volcano, across Cook Inlet from his home, sent up this mushroom cloud during its 1989-90 eruption. *(Robert Clucas)*

FACING PAGE: This volcano on the Alaska Peninsula north of Perryville honors Father Ioann Veniaminov, a Russian Orthodox missionary who became Bishop of Russian America and later Metropolitan of Moscow. Veniaminov Volcano last erupted in 1984. *(Courtesy U.S. Geological Survey)*

THE ALASKA GEOGRAPHIC SOCIETY is a non-profit organization exploring new frontiers of knowledge across the lands of the Polar Rim, putting the geography book back in the classroom, exploring new methods of teaching and learning—sharing in the excitment of discovery in man's wonderful new world north of 51°16'.

MEMBERS OF THE SOCIETY receive the ALASKA GEOGRAPHIC®, a quality magazine that devotes each quarterly issue to monographic in-depth coverage of a northern geographic region or resource-oriented subject.

MEMBERSHIP DUES in The Alaska Geographic Society are $39 per year, $43 to non-U.S. addresses. ($31.20 of the $39 yearly dues is for a one-year subscription to ALASKA GEOGRAPHIC®.) Order from The Alaska Geographic Society, P.O. Box 93370, Anchorage, AK 99509-3370; phone (907) 258-2515.

MATERIALS SOUGHT: ALASKA GEOGRAPHIC® editors seek a wide variety of informative material on the lands north of 51°16' on geographic subjects—anything to do with resources and their uses (with heavy emphasis on quality color photography)—from all the lands of the Polar Rim and the economically related North Pacific Rim. We cannot be responsible for submissions not accompanied by sufficient postage for return by certified mail. Payments for all material are made upon publication.

CHANGE OF ADDRESS: The post office does not automatically forward ALASKA GEOGRAPHIC® when you move. To ensure continuous service, notify us six weeks before moving. Send your new address and zip code, and if possible, a mailing label from a copy of ALASKA GEOGRAPHIC®, to: ALASKA GEOGRAPHIC®, P.O. Box 93370, Anchorage, Alaska 99509-3370.

MAILING LISTS: We have begun making our members' names and addresses available to carefully screened publications and companies whose products and activities may be of interest to you. If you prefer not to receive such mailings, please advise us, and include your mailing label (or your name and address if label is not available).

COLOR SEPARATIONS BY:
World of Colors USA, Inc.

PRINTED BY:
Hart Press

ABOUT THIS ISSUE: For this update of *Alaska's Volcanoes,* we called on several members of the Alaska Volcano Observatory and U.S. Geological Survey staff, especially Betsy Yount of the U.S. Geological Survey and Robert (Game) McGimsey, geologist with the Alaska Volcano Observatory. We appreciate their thorough review of the text and painstaking research, especially in preparation of charts and map and in finding photos. Dr. Tom Miller, scientist-in-charge of the observatory, updated his article on Augustine Volcano, and Dr. Jim Riehle of the survey wrote about ash deposits from Cook Inlet volcanoes. Dr. Juergen Kienle of the University of Alaska Geophysical Institute prepared the glossary of volcanic terms and made a thorough review of the text. Tom Bundtzen of the Alaska Division of Geological and Geophysical Surveys acquainted readers with Prindle Volcano in Alaska's Interior. From the original issue of *Alaska's Volcanoes* we have reprinted Ray E. Wilcox's account of Mount Spurr's 1953 eruption, Thelma Trowbridge's experience with Aniakchak's 1931 eruption and Al Keller's 1943 adventures in Okmok Caldera.

We acknowledge the efforts of Steven R. Brantley, editor of *The Eruption of Redoubt Volcano, Alaska, December 14, 1989-August 31, 1990,* (U.S. Geological Survey Circular 1061) from which the material on the Aleutian volcanic arc and Mount Redoubt is taken.

The remaining chapters were prepared by former and current members of the Alaska Geographic editorial staff.

PRICE TO NON-MEMBERS THIS ISSUE: $17.95

ISBN 0-88240-197-1

Contents

Introduction

In the 15 years since publication of the original issue of *Alaska's Volcanoes*, the Ring of Fire has continued to live up to its reputation. Led by Redoubt, Augustine, Pavlov and Veniaminov, Alaska's volcanoes have heaved and exploded, altering the north side of Augustine Island and Mount Redoubt, and showcasing a new volcanic phenomenon at Ukinrek Maars near Peulik Volcano on the Alaska Peninsula. In addition, more detailed scientific investigations of the Aleutian Range on the west

A pyroclastic flow roars down the slopes of Pavlov Volcano during this 1986 eruption. Pavlov has erupted more than 40 times since 1700. *(John Sarvis)*

side of Cook Inlet have uncovered another volcano unknown when the original issue of *Alaska's Volcanoes* was produced.

Near the remote, upper reaches of Hayes Glacier, northwest of Mount Gerdine in the Tordrillo Mountains, scientists in 1975 discovered another volcano. According to the U.S. Geological Survey, previous eruptions have destroyed much of Hayes Volcano. But investigation has shown that eruptions from there more than 3,000 years ago produced the most extensive volcanic ash layers yet found in the Cook Inlet region.

In late March 1977, an ash-laden cloud towering nearly 20,000 feet over the Peulik Volcano area first indicated that volcanic activity had once again boiled to the surface. The initial

eruption from a newly formed crater sent a sulfurous haze over Kodiak. Later, in early April, a second crater opened, showing a yellowish-orange lava lake. Ukinrek was chosen as the name for these new vents about eight miles northwest of Peulik along Bruin Bay fault.

In 1978, Westdahl, one of five active volcanoes on Unimak Island in the Aleutians, spewed more than three feet of ash on Scotch Cap. The ash damaged Scotch Cap Light and prompted evacuation of employees. This eruption created a new crater in Westdahl's summit and sent a lahar, or volcanic mud flow, sliding down the mountain's southwest flank to the sea.

In 1983 lava from Veniaminov melted an eyeglass-shaped depression

in the ice cap of the summit caldera. Residents of the fishing hamlet of Perryville reported seeing incandescent lava fountains from their ringside seat about 22 miles away on the coast.

Pavlov continues to be the most active of Alaska's volcanoes. Although weather on the Alaska Peninsula commonly hinders close observation, pilots flying to Cold Bay and the Aleutians frequently note steam and ash spewing from Pavlov's summit.

After a relatively quiet 1984 and 1985, volcanic activity increased dramatically in 1986. Pavlov, Shishaldin, Akutan, Cleveland, Makushin and Okmok throbbed and exploded. None of these eruptions, however, matched the sheer spectacle of Augustine's outburst in late March and early April.

Eruptive columns from Augustine reached more than 4,000 feet during

ABOVE: A volcanic plug survives sea, wind and temperature erosion on the east end of Amchitka Island in the Aleutians. *(Steve McCutcheon)*

RIGHT: Stream erosion exposes up to 30-foot-tall pinnacles in volcanic ash on Umnak Island. Each pinnacle was once a tubelike steam vent for degassing fumaroles through the ash. Such fumaroles were witnessed as 10,000 smokes coming out of the ash at the Katmai eruption of 1912. *(Dee Randolph)*

Alaska's Major Volcanic Centers

(Original map prepared by Dr. Juergen Kienle, University of Alaska Geophysical Institute; modifications by U.S. Geological Survey; map by Kathy Doogan)

Prindle ▲

Wrangell ▲

Spurr ▲

Redoubt ▲

Iliamna ▲

Augustine ▲

Edgecumbe

Douglas
Fourpeaked Mountain
Griggs
Kaguyak
Novarupta
Kukak
Ukinrek Maars
Denison
Peulik
Katmai
Chiginagak
Trident
Aniakchak
Mageik
Martin

Veniaminov ▲

Pavlov

Shishaldin
▲ Dana
Fisher
Dutton
Pogromni
Frosty Peak
Akutan
Roundtop Mountain
Bogoslof ▲
Isanotski Peaks
Westdahl

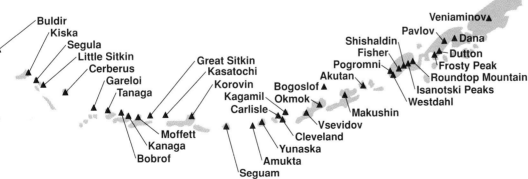

Buldir
Kiska
Segula
Little Sitkin
Cerberus
Great Sitkin
Gareloi
Kasatochi
Tanaga
Korovin
Kagamil
Carlisle
Okmok
Makushin
Moffett
Vsevidov
Kanaga
Cleveland
Bobrof
Yunaska
Amukta
Seguam

intermittent convulsions spread throughout several days. Ash blanketed communities on the western Kenai Peninsula, but winds during initial eruptions carried the main ash column north toward the Susitna Valley. Anchorage, slightly to the east of the ash plume, received only a sprinkling.

At the volcano itself, lahars ran down the south side of the mountain, and pyroclastic flows of rock particles and gases raced down the slopes at a frequency of about one every four to 10 minutes. The 1986 eruption, unlike the 1976 eruption, did not blast away the volcano's vent, rather it simply reshaped the summit dome. Later in 1986, the volcano again sent ash and steam skyward and pyroclastic flows tumbling down its slopes.

In late 1989 and through August 1990, Redoubt, Augustine's neighbor to the north, erupted for the first time since 1966. This event touched off the second most costly volcanic eruption in the nation's history, exceeded only by the 1980 Mount St. Helens explosion. The Kenai Peninsula, Anchorage bowl and much of the Matanuska-Susitna region received ash. Transportation was disrupted and an oil-loading terminal temporarily shut down.

As of spring 1991, Redoubt had been declared dormant and the rest of Alaska's volcanoes had settled down to their usual steaming, just waiting for the moment when the Ring of Fire next flashes its fury.

Alaska's Volcanoes

For three days the quiet routine of a fishing camp at Kaflia Bay, off Shelikof Strait, had been under the pall of one of nature's great cataclysmic events.

Pungent vapors were everywhere. Immense rolls of thunder echoed through an ash-blackened sky repeatedly laced by lightning. Finally, Ivan Orloff, an Aleut fisherman, could take no more. He wrote his wife:

"We are waiting for death at any moment. A mountain has burst near here. We are covered with ashes, in some places 10 feet and 6 feet deep. All this began June 6. Night and day we light lanterns. We cannot see daylight. We have no water, the rivers are just ashes mixed with water. Here are darkness and hell, thunder and noise. I do not know whether it is day or night. The earth is trembling, it lightens every minute. It is terrible. We are praying."

But Orloff, and apparently every other witness to the 1912 eruption at Katmai that produced The Valley of Ten Thousand Smokes, survived. Lack of human casualties was as remarkable as the event itself; it was one of the greatest eruptions in the Earth's history.

The terror that gripped Orloff and his contemporaries still lurks beneath the Earth's crust, as it has since before the beginning of recorded time.

Centuries ago people living on a small Mediterranean island, Vulcano, believed that Vulcano was the chimney of the forge of Vulcan, the blacksmith of the Roman gods. They thought that the hot lava fragments and clouds of dust erupting from Vulcano came from the forge as Vulcan beat out thunderbolts for Jupiter, king of the gods, and weapons for Mars, the god of war.

While scientists have now determined that volcanoes are natural phenomena, volcanology is still a frequently imprecise science. Although the eruption of a volcano can often be predicted within a few days, science cannot foretell whether a volcano will spring to life with a cataclysmic explosion or with

Classic examples of a cone altered by volcanic activity, Isanotski Peaks rise 8,025 feet on Unimak Island. *(Doug Herlihy, reprinted from ALASKA GEOGRAPHIC®)*

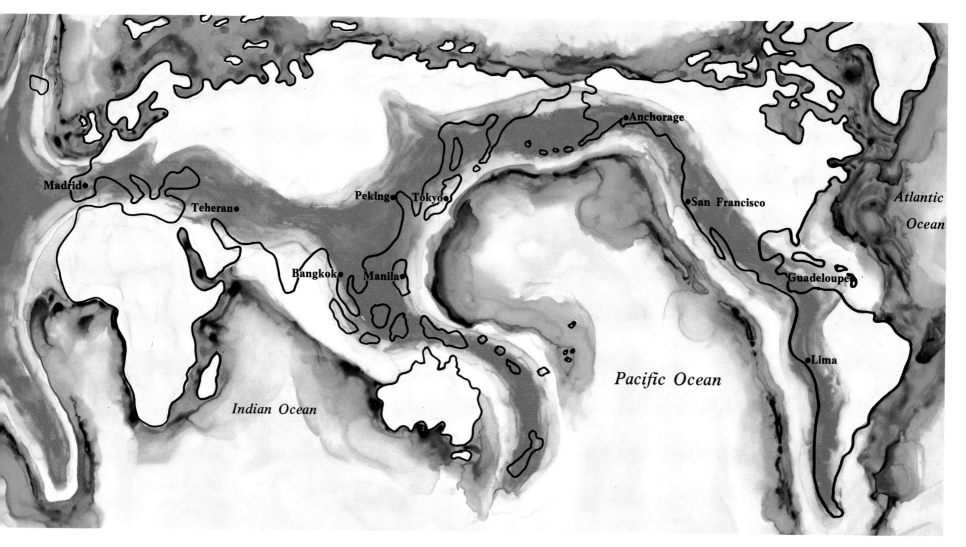

Madrid·

Teheran·

Peking· Tokyo·

·Anchorage

·San Francisco

Atlantic

Ocean

Bangkok· Manila·

Guadeloupe·

·Lima

Indian Ocean

Pacific Ocean

relatively gentle lava seeps.

Volcanoes and earthquakes have long been associated, but science has now determined that the relationship is not one of cause and effect. They are both related to a fundamental geologic process.

In recent decades, earth scientists have developed an encompassing theory that goes far toward explaining the occurrence and distribution of volcanoes and earthquakes around the world. They now believe that the surface of the Earth consists of about

a dozen major rigid plates that extend to depths of 45 miles or more and move with respect to one another at rates of several inches or more a year.

In some places, such as along the San Andreas fault in California, these plates grind past one another laterally and cause earthquakes. Along mid-ocean ridges, the plates are pushed apart along belts marked by submarine volcanism and earthquakes. Elsewhere, plates press together and one is forced beneath the other, causing both earthquakes and volcanoes at the boundary.

In southern Alaska, a plate that underlies much of the Pacific Ocean is being pushed beneath the North American Plate along the 25,000-foot-deep Aleutian Trench, causing stresses that spawn both earthquakes and volcanoes. The volcanoes are produced when parts of the upper plate are melted, and the molten material makes its way to the surface.

Most of Alaska's young volcanoes occur along an arc that extends from about Mount Spurr, 80 miles west of Anchorage, to beyond Buldir Island in the western Aleutians. The arc forms one of the most spectacular chains of volcanoes around the Pacific Basin and is this continent's major link in the basin's "Ring of Fire."

Alaska's volcanic belt on the chain contains at least 60 centers that have erupted in geologically recent times, and activity has been recorded at about 40 of these volcanoes since 1700. Some kind of volcanic event occurs along the belt almost every year.

With more than 10 percent of the world's identified volcanoes within its boundary, Alaska has become a laboratory for scientists who are trying to unravel details of the mystery of earth processes.

Surface reconnaissance by geologists has determined that older Alaska volcanoes include both shield volcanoes, largely composed of lava flows; and composite cones,

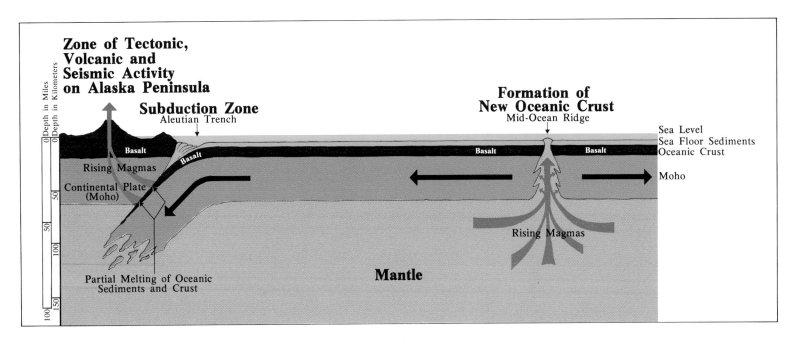

Zone of Tectonic, Volcanic and Seismic Activity on Alaska Peninsula

Depth in Miles
Depth in Kilometers

Subduction Zone
Aleutian Trench

Formation of New Oceanic Crust
Mid-Ocean Ridge

Sea Level
Sea Floor Sediments
Oceanic Crust

Basalt

Basalt

Basalt

Basalt

Moho

Rising Magmas

Continental Plate (Moho)

Rising Magmas

Partial Melting of Oceanic Sediments and Crust

Mantle

A satellite pass over the Unimak Island area shows the location of six volcanoes: Akutan, lower left; Pogromni, with Westdahl hidden on its southern flank, across Unimak Pass on the southwestern tip of Unimak Island; Shishaldin, Isanotski and Roundtop. *(NASA, reprinted from ALASKA GEOGRAPHIC®)*

mountains made up of alternate layers of lava and fragmented material. The major active volcanoes along the arc are composite cones and are of a type that make up some of the world's most beautiful mountains: Fuji in Japan, Shasta in California, Hood in Oregon and Rainier in Washington.

In the past, earth scientists had to rely on the deposits of volcanic activity to understand the event. In more recent years, however, teams of chemists, physicists and geologists have been working together at volcano observatories throughout the world in an accelerating effort to learn more

about these "windows" into the Earth.

In this country, the U.S. Geological Survey has had an observatory at Kilauea volcano in Hawaii for more than 50 years. Survey scientists keep a record of the mountain's activities, measuring the temperature and pressure of the gas emissions. Samples of lava and rocks, studies of earthquakes in the area and the volcano's magnetic field all contribute to a growing body of knowledge about volcanoes. More recently, the Survey has established observatories near Mount St. Helens and in Alaska, the latter in conjunction with the Geophysical Institute of the University of Alaska.

Augustine Volcano, in Kamishak Bay on the west side of Cook Inlet, has also been the subject of continuing scientific studies. In recent years remote sensing devices were placed around the mountain to monitor movement of magma beneath the volcano. Similar devices have been placed around the other Cook Inlet volcanoes.

RIGHT: The theory of plate tectonics states that the Earth's crust consists of several plates that float on the mantle. In some areas these plates rub against one another. The Pacific Plate is moving northward, pushing against and then diving under the North American Plate. The area where one plate moves underneath the other is called a subduction zone. Its surface manifestation is frequently a series of volcanoes such as occur in southern Alaska and the Aleutian Islands.

BELOW: Roman Leber inspects this solar-powered seismometer placed on Augustine Island after the 1986 eruption. *(Chlaus Lotscher)*

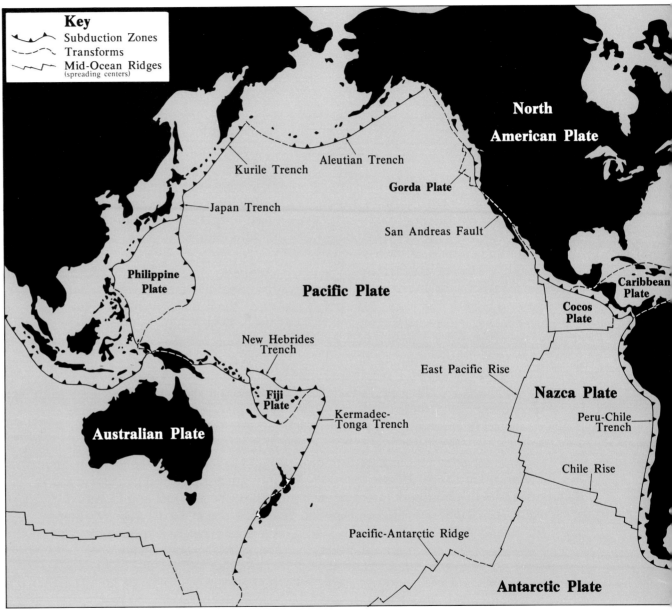

Key
Subduction Zones
Transforms
Mid-Ocean Ridges
(spreading centers)

Aleutian Trench

Kurile Trench

North American Plate

Gorda Plate

Japan Trench

San Andreas Fault

Philippine Plate

Caribbean Plate

Pacific Plate

Cocos Plate

New Hebrides Trench

East Pacific Rise

Nazca Plate

Fiji Plate

Kermadec-Tonga Trench

Peru-Chile Trench

Australian Plate

Chile Rise

Pacific-Antarctic Ridge

Antarctic Plate

Pavlov Volcano, about 40 miles northeast of Cold Bay, is the most active volcano in North America, with more than 40 eruptions logged since 1700, including this 1973 burst. *(Martin Mall, reprinted from* ALASKA GEOGRAPHIC®*)*

Knowledge gained through these and other efforts now make it possible for scientists to predict when an eruption is imminent on some long-studied volcanoes. Generally, however, particularly in remote areas such as Alaska, detailed studies of specific volcanoes are lacking and predictions are impossible.

In 1950 Robert R. Coats, of the U.S. Geological Survey, in a major study of volcanic activity along the Aleutian arc, attempted to statistically arrive at a method of predicting future volcanic activity.

By thoroughly researching technical literature, histories, diaries, letters, newspapers, and interviewing some eyewitnesses, he recorded all reported volcanic activity in Alaska from 1762 through 1948. Coats found that the most active years were 1768, 1790, 1828, 1908 and 1929, with intervals between points of high activity of 22, 38, 80 and 21 years, respectively.

Coats theorized that the statistics perhaps suggested that the higher the peak of activity, the longer the period of relative repose before the next maximum. But he questioned the validity of his data.

"For the period of the Russian occupation of Alaska, most of the recorded information concerning volcanic eruptions is in the scientific publications resulting from a very small number of exploring expeditions," he said.

"The long and nearly complete hiatus in the activity of the western volcanoes suggested by blanks in the summary from about 1830 to the first decade of this century may be merely a gap in reporting, due to the relative infrequency of travel in the western part of the arc during that period."

In addition, Coats said, weather in the area is rarely favorable for observations, and there is a continuing tendency to call the cloud that results from the condensation of water vapor "smoke." Many volcanoes continuously "steam" as meltwater from summit snow falls on internal hot spots, an event that does not presage new activity.

Coats' summary description of the study area said:

"The most conspicuous positive element in the structure of the Aleutian arc is the great curvilinear ridge extending southward and westward to Attu from the Alaskan mainland, where it merges at the northeastern end with the Alaska Range. The ridge is notably wider at the eastern end than at the western. From it a branch about 300 miles long extends northward and westward from Semisopochnoi Island, forming a submarine mountain ridge rising in places 12,000 feet above the sea floor.

"The main ridge is bounded on the north by the lowlands of the Alaska Peninsula and by the Bering Sea. The eastern part of the Bering Sea, as far west as a line extending northwestward from Unimak Pass, is very shallow. The western part of the Bering Sea is deep, and large areas of the bottom form extensive plains at depths close to 2,000 fathoms (12,000 feet). On the south, the ridge of the Aleutian Islands is bordered by the Aleutian Trench, a typical marginal deep extending to depths of about 4,200 fathoms (25,200 feet).

"In general, the volcanoes are superficial structures, built upon a basement of Tertiary [65 million years ago] and older rocks that is exposed at intervals throughout the length of the arc. The nature of the structures that have determined the position of the eruptive centers can be determined in few places.

"In detail, the volcanic line does not form a perfectly simple arc, but consists of segments of different lengths; the included angles between adjacent segments may be as little as 140°. Certain volcanoes, like Bogoslof and Amak, lie some distance away from the main line, on the concave side of the arc. In the Aniakchak region, a tension fault with an east-west trend, along or close to which several volcanic structures are aligned, has been mapped; researchers consider that the site of the eruptive center was determined by the existence of the fault. It is probable that similar relationships exist elsewhere in the arc, and that most of the volcanoes have had their sites determined by minor tensional fractures striking at an angle to the major overthrust zones. The distance of a volcano from the major active zone of movement is probably dependent upon the depth at which such a tensional fracture, originating in and limited to an overthrust block, taps eruptible magma. The minor tensional faults, by this hypothesis, bear a spatial relationship to the hypothetical major active zone.

"The distribution of earthquake foci is such that the epicenters of shallow earthquakes tend to be south of the chain; those of intermediate-depth earthquakes (deeper than 60 kilometers [96 miles]) are in the islands or north of the chain.

"The older rocks of the Aleutian arc, in some places dating back to the Paleozoic [200 to 600 million years ago] are both folded and faulted. The folding in general is relatively open, and dips are moderate. Major faults are reverse faults, trending nearly parallel to the trend of the arc; the north side has generally moved south and up with respect to the south side. In the Aniakchak area, the northwestern overthrust block has generally moved northeast and up with respect to the southeastern block. Tensional faults trending at an angle to the trend of the arc also have been noted."

Geologist Douglas Harris pans for gold in a stream draining Mount Dana ash. This volcano is the only one in the state known to have gold associated with recent eruptions. *(Courtesy of Douglas Harris)*

In spite of almost a century of study, work that has produced a much clearer understanding of the Earth's composition and its processes, there are still great gaps in the knowledge about Alaska's volcanoes. And for modern day Ivan Orloffs settled in Anchorage, Kenai, Kodiak, Cold Bay or Dutch Harbor, they are still objects of wonder and awe. And at times, of terror.

Augustine Volcano

Editor's note: *Dr. Thomas P. Miller is scientist-in-charge of the Alaska Volcano Observatory.*

Among the most spectacular of Alaska's many natural features are the more than 80 volcanoes that occur principally along the Aleutian volcanic arc and in the Wrangell Mountains. Most of these volcanoes have been active in geologically recent times, the last 1 million years, and at

On March 28, 1986, the island volcano of Augustine on the west side of Cook Inlet erupted, sending ash northeastward across parts of the Kenai Peninsula and Matanuska-Susitna basin. *(U.S. Geological Survey)*

least 40 have erupted one or more times in the past 200 years. Each year eruptions are reported from volcanoes in the Aleutian arc but are usually in such remote areas that little notice is given to them by the majority of Alaskans.

The eruption of Augustine Volcano in early 1976, however, brought a new awareness to many Alaskans of these fiery neighbors when noticeable ash fell over an area perhaps as large as 100,000 square miles.

Augustine Volcano is a symmetrical, cone-shaped feature located on uninhabited Augustine Island, named by Captain Cook in 1778, 180 miles southwest of Anchorage in lower Cook Inlet. It has been the most active volcano in the Cook Inlet region, having erupted in 1812, 1883, 1908,

1935, 1963-64, 1976 and 1986.

The eruption of 1883 was particularly violent and generated a tsunami which struck the small fishing village of English Bay 50 miles to the east on the Kenai Peninsula. The tsunami, described by witnesses as 25 to 30 feet high, fortunately came in at low tide. No lives were lost although considerable damage was done to boats and buildings.

Beginning late January 22, 1976, at least half a dozen major explosive eruptions took place during the next three days. Ash was ejected repeatedly to heights of 40,000 feet or more for durations of several minutes and formed great mushroom-shaped clouds that drifted at the whim of prevailing winds.

Between these explosive ash

At 8:30 a.m. on January 25, 1976, ash from Augustine Volcano darkens the skies of the Anchorage bowl. *(Pete Martin)*

February 6 when a new episode of explosive volcanic activity began that lasted for about 10 days. Much of the prominent volcanic dome "grown" during the 1963-64 and 1976 eruptions was destroyed during these blasts. Some time during this activity, a new dome began to appear in the summit area and grew to a height of about 850 feet. Several small ash and steam eruptions occurred during March and April.

Throughout this period, much of the volcanic activity was observed from the air; during the first few days of the eruption as many as half a dozen aircraft orbited the volcano at the same time.

To most inhabitants of southcentral Alaska, however, the most visible evidence of the volcanic eruption was a fine volcanic ash that began to fall soon after the eruption started. Ash fell over the entire Kenai Peninsula as well as in Cordova, Valdez, Anchorage and Talkeetna. The ash traveled much greater distances east and north of the volcano than west or south.

eruptions, the volcano steamed vigorously, sending billowing white clouds to heights of 10,000 feet or more. And during the major ash eruptions, hot pyroclastic flows swept down steep gullies, spreading out on the lower flanks before flowing into Cook Inlet. These pyroclastic flows consisted of turbulent mixtures of ash and gas flowing at speeds of 60 mph, with internal temperatures of more than 1,291 degrees Fahrenheit.

Temperatures of more than 1,112 degrees Fahrenheit were later measured in the area by researchers from the Geophysical Institute,

University of Alaska, at depths of only 6 feet in the material deposited by these flows.

Similar ash flows were responsible for the destruction of St. Pierre on the island of Martinique in the West Indies in 1902. The eruption of Mount Pelee caused the death of about 38,000 inhabitants; one man survived because he was in a poorly ventilated jail.

Severe thermal blasts also accompanied the pyroclastic flows of Augustine Volcano, radiating outward from its center.

Augustine Volcano seemed to be at rest from January 25, 1976, until

Once ash is injected into the atmosphere, its distribution is controlled by prevailing winds. During most of the eruptions in January and early February, the prevailing winds were from the west and southwest. A Weather Bureau satellite photo taken about 10 a.m. on January 23 showed a conspicuous ash cloud halfway across the Gulf of Alaska east of Augustine Volcano. Noticeable ash began falling on Sitka in southeastern Alaska, 680 miles from its source, later that night. No noticeable ash was reported at Kodiak, by comparison only 115 miles south of Augustine, or at King Salmon, 125 miles to the southwest.

Even greater distances traveled by Augustine ash were indicated by the detection of a dust layer of probable volcanic origin in the stratosphere over Hampton, Va., on January 28. The source of this stratospheric dust was judged by Dr. Ellis Remsberg, of NASA, to have been Augustine Volcano.

Ash began falling on the Kenai Peninsula Friday, January 23, and on the Anchorage area on Saturday morning. The falling ash on Saturday was mixed with light snow, and only gradually became apparent to Anchorage residents as they noticed a brown tinge to the newly fallen snow.

The novelty of the falling ash wore off quickly for some residents: Participants in a high school cross-country ski race found that the abrasive ash rapidly stripped the wax from their skis, and those skiers who wore contact lenses found their eyes becoming irritated as ash filtered behind the lenses. Electric utility company officials, particularly on the Kenai Peninsula, noticed increased efficiency in their natural-gas-fired turbines. The ash contained in the large quantities of air ingested by the turbines scoured a layer of corrosion off the turbine blades. Utility officials became concerned, however, about what would happen when the corroded layer was gone, and the abrasive ash began to wear down the blades themselves.

The novelty wore off even more on Sunday, January 25, when a large black cloud moved over Anchorage about 9 a.m. Ash falling from this cloud was clearly visible, and the entire Anchorage area was soon blanketed by a thin brown cover of ash. Although the ash was probably less than two-hundredths of an inch thick, it cast a dingy pallor over the entire area. Civilian and military aircraft flying through the dense ash cloud sustained considerable windshield damage.

An analysis of the ash determined that it consisted of sharp angular

Cotton-ball formations are visible in this photo of Augustine's ash cloud taken March 31, 1986, from Diamond Ridge between Homer and Anchor Point. *(Linda M. Sandlin)*

This satellite photo shows the plume from the 1986 Augustine eruption (left center) sweeping northeast across Cook Inlet to the western shore of the Kenai Peninsula, past the community of Kenai and on toward the Susitna Valley in upper Cook Inlet. *(U.S. Geological Survey; EROS Field Office)*

fragments, generally less than four-thousandths of an inch across. It was composed principally of glass and common rock-forming minerals — plagioclase, pyroxene and magnetite. It contained 63 percent silica, and was of a rock type known as dacite. In addition to the ash, Augustine also emits copious amounts of gas during an eruption, consisting chiefly of water vapor, sulfur dioxide and chlorine.

Augustine erupted again early on the morning of March 27, 1986, after several months of increased microearthquake activity. The initial four days of the eruption were very explosive with spectacular eruption plumes reaching to more than 40,000 feet and repeatedly spreading ash throughout the Cook Inlet region. Hundreds of flights in and out of Anchorage International Airport were cancelled or postponed, and minor damage was sustained by several aircraft. The U.S. Air Force evacuated most of its aircraft from Elmendorf Air Force Base for four days. Although only trace amounts of ash fell in the Anchorage area, many businesses were closed and postal delivery was cancelled on March 27.

The volcano was quiet after March 31 until April 23, when lava was extruded for five days in the summit area, forming a thick, blocky flow which draped itself over the north face of the 1976 lava dome. More lava was extruded in the summit area on August 30 and 31, after which the volcano slowly returned to its normal state although steam continues to escape from the summit area.

During all three major eruptive episodes, pyroclastic flows similar to those formed in the 1976 eruption swept down the north flank of the volcano, and in a few cases reached the sea. No massive failure of the volcano edifice occurred, and no tsunami was generated. The possibility of such an event, however, will always be a matter of concern during Augustine eruptions.

Although the 1986 eruption of Augustine was similar — and perhaps even slightly smaller — than the 1976 eruption, it was far more disruptive to southcentral Alaska residents. In part this was because of an increase in population and air traffic, but it also probably reflected the impact of the 1980 Mount St. Helens eruption on the public's awareness of volcanic hazards. Too often such awareness fades rapidly away as time goes on; in the case of Augustine and other Cook Inlet volcanoes, however, the hazard remains.

The frequency of eruptions from Augustine Volcano strongly suggests that molten material, or magma, lies close to the Earth's surface below Augustine Island. Periodically, this magma and associated gases work their way to the surface.

Long-range predictions of future Augustine eruptions are impossible. The occurrence of six major eruptions in the past 105 years, however, indicates the general time frame in which future eruptions should be expected. The intervals between these eruptions have been as short as 10 years and as long as 33 years. Many Alaskans will certainly see Augustine Volcano erupt again.

Short-range predictions of volcanic eruptions are, however, becoming feasible. The movement of molten material high into a volcanic cone is usually accompanied by seismic disturbances. Seismographs can detect these precursor earth movements and often give up to several days' advance warning of an impending eruption. A net of seismic stations, installed by the University of Alaska, had monitored

A fast-moving pyroclastic flow roars down the steep upper slopes of Augustine Volcano. Sometimes moving at speeds of many miles per hour, pyroclastic flows contain rock particles, volcanic gases and entrapped air that fall out of the eruptive column and run down the side of the volcano. Heated to temperatures of 1,100 to 1,300 degrees, the gases in this turbulent material expand, winnowing out the finer-grained particles. This causes the billowing clouds characteristic of a pyroclastic flow. *(U.S. Geological Survey)*

seismic activity on Augustine Island for about five years but quit transmitting in the few weeks prior to the 1976 eruption. The seismic net was reestablished, however, and allowed warnings to be given prior to the 1986 eruption. By 1991 the Alaska Volcano Observatory maintained five seismic and two tilt meter stations on the island with real time data transmission to Fairbanks. A tilt meter detects inflation of the volcanic cone by magma.

Most of Alaska's young volcanoes occur along a belt that extends from near Mount Spurr, 80 miles west of Anchorage, to beyond Buldir Island in the western Aleutians and are noted as prominent landmarks. Spurr, Redoubt and Iliamna volcanoes on the west side of Cook Inlet, for example, can easily be seen from Anchorage on a clear day. All three of these volcanoes have had historic eruptions and have active steam vents. Indeed, in July 1953, a parasitic cone on the south flank of Mount Spurr suddenly erupted and in a matter of a few hours ash began falling on Anchorage. By noon the ash cloud was so thick that it caused the automatically controlled street light system to go on.

Certain volcanoes have been particularly consistent performers. Both Pavlov, near the tip of the Alaska Peninsula, and Shishaldin, 80 miles to the west on Unimak Island, have erupted more than 25 times in the past 200 years and as recently as 1988. Shishaldin is judged to be one of the most beautifully symmetrical volcanic cones in the world, rivaling the classical cone of Mount Fuji in Japan. It has a basal diameter of 8 miles and rises to almost 10,000 feet.

Much of the historic volcanic activity in southern Alaska has taken the form of ash eruptions rather than lava flows. This is opposite of the situation in Hawaii, where lava flows predominate, reflecting the different geologic settings, gas content and

Abrasive ash and other airborn particles from the 1986 eruption of Augustine Volcano forced air traffic to shut down at Anchorage International Airport and at other airports on the Kenai Peninsula. Utility company officials were concerned that volcanic emissions might harm their turbine generators; thus some businesses in Anchorage, about 180 miles to the northeast, closed early on March 27 to decrease the use of electricity. *(Tom Walker)*

Ash from Augustine's 1986 eruption dusts these cars parked along a street in Homer. The island volcano, easily seen from Homer on clear days, rises from Cook Inlet on the edges of Kamishak Bay. *(Tom Walker)*

chemical composition of the volcanic materials of the two regions.

The most spectacular of all historic Alaskan eruptions occurred in early June 1912, when more than 6 cubic miles of ash and pumice, weighing more than 33,000 million tons, was ejected from Novarupta vent near the base of Mount Katmai in what is now Katmai National Park and Preserve.

Thousands of square miles on the Alaska Peninsula and nearby Kodiak Island were covered by ash; more than 50 feet was deposited near Mount Katmai and 10 inches at Kodiak, 110 miles away. The noise of the explosive eruption was heard 600 miles away. One of the side effects of this eruption was the ejection of a turbulent mixture of ash, pumice and gas, known as an ash flow, that moved like a heavy fluid 14 miles down a northwest-trending valley from Novarupta. These earlier ash flows were similar in content, but exceeded by far the volume thrown out of Augustine in 1986.

Although most of Alaska's volcanoes occur along the Aleutian volcanic arc, geologically young volcanoes are also found in the Wrangell Mountains, southeastern Alaska and western Alaska. Some of the world's highest volcanoes are part of the Wrangells including 16,000-foot Mount Sanford. In the area, however, Mount Wrangell is the only volcano showing any activity; it has a vigorously steaming crater in its ice-filled summit caldera. Observations by University of Alaska Geophysical Institute researchers confirm that the amount of heat in the summit area has been increasing for the past 25 years. Whether this increase forecasts an impending eruption is unknown. Two violent explosive eruptions did occur in the eastern Wrangells, near the Canadian border, about 1,900 and 1,300 years ago, and deposited large amounts of ash over 125,000 square miles of eastern Alaska and Yukon Territory.

Mount Edgecumbe, near Sitka in southeastern Alaska, currently shows no sign of activity, but it is thought to have been the source of the volcanic ash deposited about 10,000 years ago as far north as Glacier Bay.

About 10,000 square miles of western and interior Alaska are covered by lava flows, some as young as a few hundred years old. The sources of these lava flows are low cones and fissures, none of which are as spectacular as the towering volcanoes of southern Alaska.

Volcanoes are a prominent part of the Alaskan landscape and will continue to be. Each year one or more of these volcanoes can be expected to put on a spectacular display of fiery activity that cannot fail to awe those who witness it.

Mount Katmai

In early June 1912, the three-peaked spire known as Mount Katmai, after apparently centuries of quiescence, burst in an eruption that was the greatest volcanic catastrophe in the recorded history of Alaska.

More than 6 cubic miles of ash and pumice, estimated to have a total weight of more than 33,000 million tons, were blown into the air from the mountain and adjacent vents in an area now known as The Valley of Ten

A solitary hiker crosses a portion of the ash flow in Katmai's Valley of Ten Thousand Smokes. In June 1912, the area around Mount Katmai and Novarupta exploded, sending forth more than 6 cubic miles of ash. *(Harry M. Walker)*

Thousand Smokes. Later measurements of thickness of ash led to a conclusion that almost all of the material was erupted from smaller vents in the valley and a new volcano, Novarupta; and that Mount Katmai played a subordinate role in a series of eruptions.

Modern researchers have suggested that the relationship between Mount Katmai and Novarupta was that of a storage vessel and relief valve. Novarupta's base is located thousands of feet in elevation below Katmai, and some authorities now believe that a fissure system, newly formed at the time, stretched across the intervening six miles and connected the two underground. It drained Katmai's reservoir to the point where the mountain could not support its own

weight and collapsed, creating a mile-deep caldera that measured more than three miles in diameter. For more than a quarter of a century the most complete account of the eruption at Mount Katmai was that prepared by Dr. Robert F. Griggs, an Ohio State University botanist, who led four expeditions into the area in the years immediately following the eruption. His efforts to reconstruct events preceding the eruption were hampered by a lack of on-scene witnesses, and fragmentary bits of information about the eruption itself were often seemingly in conflict.

Dr. Griggs missed the significance of Novarupta in the explosive chain of events. But his detailed investigation was able to determine that as much as five days before the eruption,

BELOW: Stark reminders of the once-thick vegetation in the area, these members of the Ukak "Ghost Forest" at the mouth of Ukak River were killed by hot mud flow from the Novarupta eruption. *(Michael Funke)*

RIGHT: This map indicates the limits of major damage caused by the Katmai eruption. Original source data shows no damage on the island in Amalik Bay. *(U.S. Geological Survey, reprinted from ALASKA GEOGRAPHIC®)*

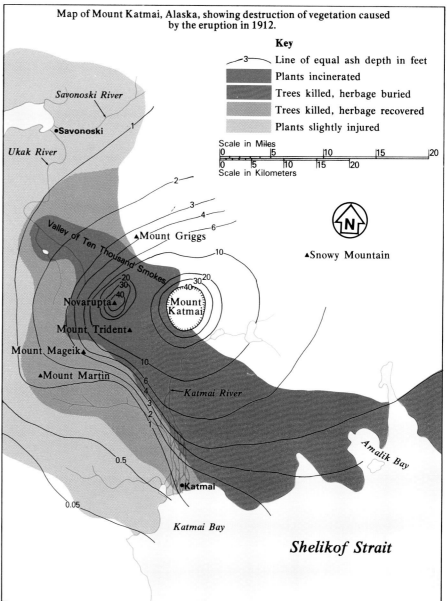

Map of Mount Katmai, Alaska, showing destruction of vegetation caused by the eruption in 1912.

Key
—3—— Line of equal ash depth in feet
Plants incinerated
Trees killed, herbage buried
Trees killed, herbage recovered
Plants slightly injured

Scale in Miles
Scale in Kilometers

Savonoski River
•Savonoski
Ukak River

Valley of Ten Thousand Smokes
▲Mount Griggs
▲Snowy Mountain
Novarupta▲
Mount Katmai
Mount Trident▲
Mount Mageik▲
▲Mount Martin
Katmai River
Amalik Bay
•Katmai
Katmai Bay
Shelikof Strait

A lake now fills the summit caldera of 6,715-foot Mount Katmai. *(Michael Funke)*

earthquakes began at Katmai village, 20 miles from the volcano. Villagers became frightened and on June 4 moved to a camp 10 miles down the coast. When the eruption broke out June 5, they proceeded another 20 miles along the coast to Puale Bay. About the same time, villagers at Savonoski, about 20 miles northwest of Mount Katmai, also became frightened and made their way to Naknek, 50 miles away.

On the evening of June 5 an eruptive cloud was reportedly seen from Puale Bay, and during the morning of June 6 several large explosions were heard. At about 1 p.m., the same day, the great explosions of the main phase of the eruption began and continued for more than two days. Major explosions occurred at about 3 p.m. and 11 p.m., June 6 and around 11 p.m., June 7.

Fragmentary accounts at the time suggest that fairly strong eruptions continued for several weeks, after which the amount of ash being erupted diminished, although earth tremors and gas-laden explosions continued for several months.

No seismographs recorded the preliminary earthquakes, but quakes accompanying the first few days of the eruption itself, however, were picked up by recording devices in Victoria, British Columbia, and in Seattle. Air shock waves of the explosions were reported to have been seen from Seldovia, 150 miles away, and the noises to have been heard at Juneau, 750 miles from the site.

After long study Dr. Griggs was to summarize his understanding of the sequence of events at the time of the eruption by saying:

"Just before Mount Katmai exploded, the valley, through which ran the old trail across the peninsula, burst open in many places, and a great mass of incandescent material poured through the fissures. This molten magma was surcharged with gases like the distinctive clouds which emanated from Mt. Pelee. Flowing

down the valley under gravity, it filled an area more than 50 square miles in extent with a deposit of fine ground tuff.

"After the extension of solid material, the valley continued to emit gases in great volume, forming millions of fumaroles, which constitute one of the most awe-inspiring spectacles. This feature . . . was discovered by the expedition . . . in 1916 . . . and named 'The Valley of Ten Thousand Smokes.'"

In an effort to set the effects of the eruption in a more familiar context, Dr. Griggs later reported:

"If such an eruption should occur on Manhattan Island, the column of steam would be conspicuous as far as Albany. The sounds of the explosions would be plainly audible in Chicago. The fumes would sweep over all states east of the Rocky Mountains. In Denver they would tarnish exposed brass, and even linen hung out on the line would be so eaten by the sulphuric acid content as to fall to pieces on the ironing board. As far away as Toronto the acid raindrops

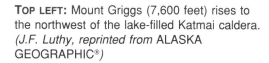

TOP LEFT: Mount Griggs (7,600 feet) rises to the northwest of the lake-filled Katmai caldera. *(J.F. Luthy, reprinted from* ALASKA GEOGRAPHIC®*)*

LEFT: "Just before Mount Katmai exploded, the valley, through which ran the old trail across the peninsula, burst open in many places, and a great mass of incandescent material poured through the fissures. This molten magma was surcharged with gasses. . . . Flowing down the valley under gravity, it filled an area more than 50 square miles in extent with a deposit if fine ground tuff," explained Dr. Robert F. Griggs, leader of the first scientific team to visit The Valley of Ten Thousand Smokes after the 1912 eruption. *(Penny Rennick)*

would cause stinging burns wherever they fell on face or hands.

"Ash would accumulate in Philadelphia a foot deep. To add to the terrors of the catastrophe, that city would grope for sixty hours in total darkness — darkness blacker than anything imaginable, so thick that a lantern held at arm's length could not be seen.

"As for the horrors that would be enacted along the lower Hudson, no detailed picture may be drawn. There would be no occasion for rescue work, for there would be no survivors. The whole of Manhattan Island, and an equal area besides, would open in great yawning chasms, and fiery fountains of molten lava would issue from every crack.

"This, disrupted by the escaping gases, would be changed into red hot sand, which, consuming everything it touched, would run like wildfire through the town. The flow of incandescent sand would effectually destroy all evidence of the former city. In its deepest parts, the near-molten sand would probably overtop the tallest skyscrapers."

Dr. Griggs' graphic description, to a large degree, was an extension of the information he discovered in the logs of two ships cruising in Alaska waters at the time of the eruptions.

The U.S. revenue cutter *Manning* spearheaded relief work at Kodiak following the 1912 Katmai eruption. *(Alaska Historical Library, reprinted from ALASKA GEOGRAPHIC®)*

On June 6 the steamer *Dora* was moving through Shelikof Strait bound for Kodiak, and Captain C.B. McMullen noted in the ship's log:

"Left Uyak at 8:15 a.m., a strong westerly breeze and fine clear weather. At 1 o'clock p.m. while entering Kupreanot Straits [Kupreanof Strait], sighted a heavy cloud of smoke directly astern, raising from the Alaska Peninsula. I took a bearing of same, which I made out to be Katmai Volcano, distance about 55 miles away. The smoke arose and spread in the sky following the vessel, and by 3:00 p.m. was directly over us, having travelled at the rate of 20 miles an hour.

"At 6:00 p.m. passed through Uzmka Narrows [Narrow Strait], fine and clear ahead, and continued on expecting to make Kodiak. At 6:30 p.m. when off Spruce Rock, which is about 3 1/2 miles from Mill Bay Rocks and the entrance to Kodiak, ashes commenced to fall and in a few minutes we were in complete darkness, not even the water over the ship's side could be seen.

"I continued on in the hopes that I might pick up entrance to Kodiak, but when the vessel had run the distance by the log, conditions were the same, so I decided to head out to sea and get clear of all danger. At 7:22 p.m. I set a course of northeast by north (magnetic). Wind commenced to increase rapidly now from the southeast and the vessel was driven before it. Heavy thunder and lightning commenced early in the afternoon and continued throughout the night. Birds of all species kept falling on the deck in a helpless condition. The temperature rose owing to the heat of the volcanic ash, the latter penetrating into all parts of the ship, even down into the engine room.

"About 4:30 a.m. next day vessel cleared the black smoke, emerging

Knife Creek cuts through hundreds of feet of volcanic ash in Katmai National Park and Preserve. Dubbed The Valley of Ten Thousand Smokes by National Geographic teams that studied the area in several expeditions from 1915 to 1919, the valley can be reached today by van from the park's headquarters at Brooks Camp on Naknek Lake. *(Harry M. Walker)*

into a fiery red haze, which turned yellow, and by 6:00 a.m. the ashes ceased to fall and the horizon was clear from west to north."

Captain K.W. Perry, in the June 7 log entry of the U. S. revenue cutter *Manning*, at Kodiak reported:

"All streams and wells have now become choked, about five inches of ash having fallen, and water was furnished inhabitants by the *Manning* and by a schooner.

"At noon ashes began to fall again, increased until 1:00 p.m., visibility was 50 feet. Abject terror took possession of the place. At 2:00 p.m. pitch darkness shut in. There were heavy static disturbances to the radio. No light appeared at dawn June 8. Ash had been removed from the ship June 7, but now decks, masts, yards, and lifeboats were loaded with flakes of fine dust of a yellowish color. Sulphurous fumes came at times in the air. Avalanches of ashes could be heard sliding on the neighboring hills sending forth clouds of suffocating dust. The crew kept at work with shovels, and four streams of water were kept playing incessantly to try to rid the ship of ash. The dust fall was so heavy that a lantern could not be seen at arm's length."

As indicated by the logs, ashfall of the eruption was mainly in the quadrant east-southeastward across Kodiak Island, with a minor lobe to the north.

According to Griggs' detailed studies, an area of 3,000 square miles was covered by ash a foot or more deep, and 30,000 square miles by more than an inch of ash. Small ashfalls were also recorded in Fairbanks, 500 miles away, Juneau, 750 miles distant, and in the Puget Sound region, about 1,500 miles away.

Appreciable amounts of extremely fine ash blown into the stratosphere remained suspended for months, causing spectacular red sunsets in many parts of the globe. The ash-laden atmosphere, because of its ability to reflect radiant heat from the sun, also reportedly reduced average world temperatures about 34 degrees during the following year. And some scientists have theorized that the highly unlikely event of a series of eruptions like that at Katmai could bring on a new ice age.

Largely because of Dr. Griggs' studies, and the active interest of the National Geographic Society, which funded his field investigations, Katmai was set aside as a national monument by presidential order in 1918. On December 2, 1980, Katmai became a national park and preserve of 4.2 million-plus acres.

Aleutian Volcanic Arc

Redoubt Volcano lies near the northeast end of the Aleutian volcanic arc, an active chain of volcanoes that extends 1,550 miles from near Anchorage southwest along the Alaska Peninsula to the western Aleutian Islands. At least one volcano in the chain erupts, on average, each year. Scientists have identified more than 40 historically active volcanic centers along the chain, and they are particularly concerned about volcanoes whose eruptions could affect the Cook Inlet region, where about 60 percent of Alaska's population resides and which is the state's major supply, business and financial center. Three volcanoes west of Cook Inlet — Spurr, Redoubt and Augustine — have erupted ash over Cook Inlet population centers seven times since 1900. Recently, geologists identified about 90 different layers of volcanic ash in the upper Cook Inlet region that formed during the past 10,000 years. These layers record only a small percentage of the eruptions scientists think have occurred during this time. At least 30 of the layers are attributed to eruptions of Redoubt, and 35 layers are attributed to the Crater Peak vent on nearby Mount Spurr.

[*From* The Eruption Of Redoubt Volcano, Alaska, December 14, 1989 - August 31, 1990 *(1990)]*

Lying near the shore of Becharof Lake in Becharof National Wildlife Refuge, Ukinrek Maars, among the newest of Alaska's volcanoes, erupts steam and gas on April 5, 1977. *(Steve McCutcheon)*

Redoubt Blows

Editor's note: *This summary of the most recent major eruption of Redoubt Volcano is taken in part from U.S. Geological Survey Circular 1061,* The Eruption Of Redoubt Volcano, Alaska, December 14, 1989, - August 31, 1990. *(1990), edited by Steven R. Brantley.*

The 1989-90 eruption of Redoubt Volcano, 100 miles southwest of Anchorage, began December 14, 1989, less than 24 hours after a swarm of earthquakes struck beneath the

Redoubt Volcano towers over the upper Drift River valley. *(Cynthia Gardner, Alaska Volcano Observatory)*

volcano. A huge cloud of ash heralded the volcano's fourth and most damaging eruption of this century. Volcanic ash generated by numerous explosive episodes from December 1989 through April 1990 caused significant damage to aircraft, severely disrupted air traffic above southern Alaska and resulted in local power outages and school closures. The explosions produced hot, fast-moving clouds of ash, rock debris and gas (pyroclastic flows) that swept across Redoubt's heavily glaciated north flank. These events triggered massive debris flows in Drift River valley that threatened an oil tanker terminal near the river's mouth. Partial flooding of the terminal compound on two occasions forced authorities to modify the terminal's

operating procedures, which temporarily curtailed oil production from 10 platforms in Cook Inlet. The damage and loss of revenue from ash and debris flows are estimated to total more than $100 million, which makes this the second most costly eruption in the history of the United States, exceeded only by the 1980 eruption of Mount St. Helens in Washington.

The eruption not only focused public attention on the hazards posed by Redoubt Volcano and other volcanoes in the Cook Inlet region, but also demonstrated the value of monitoring volcanoes and the capability of providing forecasts of impending eruptions. The recently established Alaska Volcano Observatory (AVO), a consortium of the U.S. Geological Survey, the Geophysical

Institute of the University of Alaska and the Alaska Division of Geological and Geophysical Surveys, monitors active volcanoes west of Cook Inlet to detect signs of volcanic unrest that may lead to an eruption and conducts geologic studies to assess the hazards the volcanoes pose. A seismic network centered on Redoubt became fully operational in October 1989 as part of

One of the victims of Mount Redoubt's 1989-90 eruptions was the Drift River Oil Terminal, 20 miles from the volcano on the west side of Cook Inlet at the mouth of Drift River. Debris loosened by Redoubt's volcanic activity pushed down Drift River, dropped some of its material when it reached the wider channel of the lower river, and moved laterally to flood Rust Slough, twisting by on the left side of the terminal. These events endangered the terminal's storage tanks, which can contain 1.9 billion barrels of oil and which held more than 800,000 barrels when the eruption began in December 1989.
(Alaska Volcano Observatory)

the AVO monitoring program. This seismic network and detailed observations, plus experience gained by scientists monitoring eruptions in the 1980s at Mount St. Helens, Nevado del Ruiz in Columbia and Augustine Volcano, enabled AVO to provide accurate information about Redoubt's activity and to issue advance warnings for several explosive episodes.

Highlights of the Eruption and Monitoring

The activity of Redoubt during the first nine months of the 1989-90 eruption was not as violent — and did not produce as much erupted material — as some other eruptions in

the world in this century; nor were effects of this activity unexpected. Nevertheless, monitoring Redoubt's activity provided valuable lessons for mitigating volcanic hazards in the future.

Principal observations include:

◆ The explosive onset of the eruption on December 14 was preceded by only about 24 hours of intense seismic activity. Because the volcano was being monitored, this was sufficient time for AVO to warn officials and the public of Redoubt's restlessness, and for AVO and other government agencies to activate emergency plans before eruptive activity began.

◆ Increases in the rate of seismicity beneath the volcano were the basis for short-term warnings issued before major eruptions on December 14 and January 2 and before moderate eruptions on March 23 and April 6. AVO monitored seismic activity beneath Redoubt 24 hours a day to enable scientists both to alert aviation and public officials of the increased potential for ash and debris flows and to determine when such events were happening, especially at night and when clouds obscured the volcano. Not all significant episodes were forecast, however, because a seismic station on the volcano was destroyed early in the eruption sequence and because detectable changes in seismicity did not precede some of the smaller explosions.

♦ The size and type of volcanic activity that occurred during the 1989-90 eruption typified Redoubt's past activity as inferred from the geologic record. Analysis of hazards based on a volcano's eruptive history can be used in long-term planning and investment in volcanic areas. The Drift River Oil Terminal was built in 1967, before such a hazard assessment was initiated.

♦ Volcanic ash is the most common and widespread volcanic hazard in Alaska; it is especially dangerous to aircraft. At least four commercial jets suffered damage from encounters with airborne ash during the eruption's first three months. On December 15 a Boeing 747 jetliner carrying 231 passengers entered an ash cloud 150 miles northeast of Redoubt. The jet lost power in all four engines and dropped about 12,000 feet in altitude before the pilot succeeded in restarting the engines. The plane landed safely in Anchorage, but sustained an estimated $80 million

in damage. Although existing technology cannot always track the movement of ash away from a volcano, this incident prompted AVO and other agencies to search for ways to better inform the airline industry about wind direction and speed and eruptive activity.

♦ Numerous floods of water, ice and volcanic-rock debris (debris flows) inundated the Drift River valley when explosions disturbed portions of Redoubt's cover of snow and ice. Pyroclastic flows swept across Drift River glacier and eroded and melted several hundred million cubic feet of snow and glacial ice, generating water that combined with sediment to cause massive debris flows. The largest debris flows, on January 2 and February 15, entered Drift River terminal from Rust Slough and damaged its logistical support facilities. No oil, however, was spilled.

♦ New experimental systems were effective in detecting large ash plumes

Steam still swirls from the cooling lava dome over the vent at the 6,200-foot level of Mount Redoubt in July 1990. *(David Wieprecht, courtesy Alaska Volcano Observatory)*

and volcanic debris flows. Lightning discharges associated with several large plumes of ash were detected with a system designed for locating cloud-to-ground strikes, and debris flows in the upper Drift River valley were detected by an array of seismometers especially sensitive to high-frequency vibrations of the ground.

Mount Spurr

By Ray E. Wilcox

Editor's note: *This article was written several years ago for the original issue of* Alaska's Volcanoes. *Ray Wilcox is a geologist, now retired, with the U.S. Geological Survey.*

At 5 a.m. July 9, 1953, a glacier-filled vent on the south flank of Mount Spurr erupted with tremendous violence, shooting a mushroom cloud to a height of 60,000 to 70,000 feet in 40 minutes.

By chance the eruption was

In 1953 Mount Spurr, 80 miles west of Anchorage, erupted, sending an ash cloud over the Anchorage bowl and much of the surrounding area. *(Steve McCutcheon)*

witnessed from its onset by pilots whose photos and descriptions provided a valuable record of this type of eruption.

The bulk of material of the eruption was blown out in only a few brief surges on July 9, and was carried due eastward across Cook Inlet and over the city of Anchorage, 80 miles away. No lava flows occurred, and during the next few weeks the eruption subsided to a weak emission of steam.

The outbreak did not take place at the summit, but at a point about 7,000 feet above sea level on the south shoulder of the mountain just above the Chakachatna River Gorge. No historic record of eruptions of this or other vents on Mount Spurr prior to 1953 are known, except for minor emissions of steam in 1927.

In 1953 the only recognized symptom that suggested an impending eruption was increased fumarolic activity in the peak area noted by pilots during the latter part of May. The seismic record at Fairbanks, 300 miles northeast of Mount Spurr, showed that for the evening of July 8, and early hours of July 9, several brief disturbances occurred that may or may not have been connected with the imminent eruption. Because of their relatively short oscillation periods, which is characteristic of volcanic (local) quakes, it seems entirely possible that they may have been precursors of the eruption, although no epicenter distance determinations have been made on the records of these quakes. At a few minutes before 5 a.m. on July 9, the

Spurr's ash blanketed much of southcentral Alaska and proved difficult to remove from houses. (Anchorage Times, *reprinted from* ALASKA GEOGRAPHIC®)

seismograph began recording swarms of confused "microseisms," vibrations of small intensity and short duration, that were quite different in character from microseisms associated with normal earthquakes.

The following pilot's account of the initial phase of the eruption was released by the U. S. Air Force July 10, 1953:

"At 05h 05m Lieutenant Metzner noticed a column of smoke 60 miles ahead that was about 15,000 feet high and one-eighth mile wide. As he approached the smoke it was apparent that the eruption causing it was becoming increasingly severe with the smoke growing rapidly in height. At about 25 miles distance, the volcano was recognized as Mount Spurr. Both planes approached the mountain at about 15,000 feet and circled the volcano at about 05h 25m. They noticed the continuing increase in the intensity and size of the column of smoke with lightning flashes through its core every 30 seconds. Smoke issued from the volcano in violent billows at the 7,000-foot level of the mountain caused by huge subterranean explosions. Tremors on the mountainsides were visible from the aircraft and were followed by snow slides on the mountain. The smoke had by now reached the 30,000-foot level, rolling upward and assuming the shape of the atomic bomb mushroom. Clouds of smoke were every shade of gray from black at the crater to pure white at the top. By this time the width had increased to about a mile at the base and 30 miles at its widest part.

"About 05h 40m Lieutenant Metzner climbed in order to estimate the height of the mushroom. The top of the stalk, or the bottom of the mushroom, was 30,000 feet and the top of the mushroom had climbed to 70,000 feet. Lightning was now flashing from top to bottom of the mushroom at three second intervals.

"At about 06h 00m volcanic ash began falling from the mushroom on all sides and finally made the entire area hazy. A clear definition of the volcano and the mushroom rapidly faded and the patrol returned to its base."

Wind from the west carried the great sinking ash umbrella due eastward and allowed practically no ash to fall on the west side of the volcano. At 9 a.m. a pilot reported ash still being erupted in great quantities, but another observation at noon reported decreased activity. A resumption of strong activity was reported at 3:30 p.m., and other eruptions apparently took place during the afternoon or evening.

The "microseismic" activity recorded at Fairbanks, which had begun in earnest just before 5 a.m., increased in intensity until about 9 a.m., then diminished rapidly to normal levels. A similar disturbance began again at about 3:30 p.m., built to a climax by 5 p.m., and thereafter subsided rapidly. The coincidence of times of seismic disturbance and observed periods of strong explosive eruption leave little doubt that this peculiar seismic activity originated at Mount Spurr.

The ash cloud of the first eruptive surges of July 9 moved slowly eastward and by 11 a.m. the leading edge of the descending mushroom, by now greatly distorted, had spread out above Anchorage. While ash fell heavily on the northwest shore of Cook Inlet, it was not yet falling in Anchorage, and the base of the ash cloud sloped upward to the east in its direction of movement. Fine ash started falling in Anchorage shortly before noon, when darkness caused the automatic switching system to turn on the street lights, and continued to fall copiously until 3 p.m. After that the rate of ash fall decreased but some continued through the night. By early morning only a pall of dust hung over the area.

At 5 the next morning the vent was only steaming. But at 3:30 p.m. an especially strong surge of ash-laden steam rose to 20,000 feet. From July 11 to 16, the eruption consisted only of white steam clouds rising to maximum altitudes of 20,000 feet and occasional puffs of black dust and rock debris, most of which fell back into the throat of the volcano.

A mudflow or debris-laden flood must have occurred July 9 or 10, because investigators arriving at the volcano July 11 found a fresh debris dam across the Chakachatna River just below the vent and a new 5-mile-long lake. The mudflow may have been caused by the torrential rains of the initial eruption or by meltwater from the ice that apparently had filled the vent prior to the eruption.

The zone of heavy ashfall covered an area about 25 miles wide extending almost due eastward from Mount Spurr. Thickest ash and lapilli deposits were not far from the volcano. At Anchorage the deposit was variously one-eighth to one-fourth-inch thick, decreasing to the east where some minor ashfall was reported at Valdez and within 30 miles of Cordova, 200 miles from the volcano. Additional reports of ashfall came from Kenai, Kalgin Island and as far south along Cook Inlet as Tuxedni Bay, 80 miles south of Mount Spurr, near Iliamna.

Anchorage Daily Times newsboys donned surplus military masks to combat the ash-laden air. Early headlined reports were incorrect. (Anchorage Times, *reprinted from* ALASKA GEOGRAPHIC®)

41

Volcanic Ash in the Cook Inlet Region

By Jim Riehle

Editor's note: *Dr. Jim Riehle is a volcanologist with the Branch of Alaskan Geology, U.S. Geological Survey, and has studied extensively Alaska's volcanic ash deposits.*

Long-term residents of south-central Alaska are familiar with the temporary effects of light volcanic ashfalls: irritation of the respiratory tract, abrasion of machinery and pollution of surface water. Prehistoric deposits of volcanic ash in the region

Footprints across Anchorage's Park Strip trample an unblemished carpet of ash-covered snow from Augustine's 1976 eruption. (Pete Martin)

provide important information about eruptions of Cook Inlet volcanoes and indicate that some past eruptions were much larger than historic ones. What is volcanic ash, and how do geologists use it to study volcanoes?

Ash is any sand-sized particle ejected by a volcano. The term probably originated by analogy to the warm fragments that float down from smoke plumes of fires. The scientific term is *tephra*, the Greek word for hot, fragmented material erupted by a volcano. Some material making up ash is old pieces of the volcano that were broken by, and accidentally caught in, the eruption. These accidental fragments are typically not hot because most of them were heated only just before, or in, the explosion. Some eruptions produce only

accidental ash. These eruptions are commonly the indirect result of magma buried within a volcano; such buried magma usually requires centuries to a few millennia to cool. While cooling, the magma heats surrounding rocks and groundwater in the rocks. The heated groundwater can leak from the ground in hot springs, or it can build up pressure beneath the ground to suddenly erupt as steam and accidental ash. Steam eruptions are typically of short duration and small volume because the amount of energy available in heated groundwater is small. Also, steam eruptions are difficult to predict because they need not be accompanied by lengthy or obvious warnings, such as earthquakes large enough to be detected away from the volcano.

More exciting is a second type of ash fragment: juvenile ash consisting of chilled pieces of magma. Magma is melted rock, and its eruption at the ground is the basic reason for volcanoes. Juvenile fragments in ash signify that new magma has worked its way close to the surface. The arrival of magma at the surface can lead to a lengthy phase of large eruptions; because of its high temperature, the amount of energy in magma that is potentially available to eruptions is much more than in steam eruptions. Many eruptive episodes begin with steam eruptions when new magma first works its way low into the volcano, and later give way to magmatic eruptions after the magma has risen higher.

Distinguishing accidental from juvenile ash fragments is normally not difficult. Magma is a mixture of melted rock and new mineral grains that grow by cooling of the magma as it works its way to the surface. The residual magma between the mineral grains holds dissolved gases, chiefly water and forms of nitrogen and carbon, that drive the eruption by their explosive expansion as the magma decompresses during its rise. The expanding gases form bubbles in the magma, which are preserved when the magma erupts and chills in the air to form glass. Bubbled glass is the essential characteristic of juvenile ash. If the bubbles are small and plentiful, the result is pumice, a type of bubbled glass. Pumice is light enough to float on water.

Glass causes the abrasiveness of juvenile ash. Like pieces of broken window glass, juvenile ash has sharp points and edges that irritate mucous membranes, abrade metal and acquire static charges. Volcanic glass reverts to a sticky fluid upon heating to only about 1,200 degrees. Thus mineral grains in an ash cloud, which melt at higher temperatures, can pass through jet engines but glass coats turbine blades. This coating, aided by oxygen starvation upon intake of gas in the ash plume, has caused engine failure in several recent cases where jet aircraft flew into ash plumes.

Thus the appearance of glass in succeeding ash eruptions signals to geologists that the volcano may be entering a period of explosive magmatic eruptions. And volcanic glass is the primary basis by which geologists can determine which prehistoric ash deposits at separate sites are likely to be deposits of the same ashfall, and which volcano is the source. Occasionally an uncommon mineral type is unique to a particular volcano, but generally the mineral grains in ash deposits are common to all the volcanoes of the region, and thus are useless as indicators of source. Repeated observations have shown, however, that the chemical composition of volcanic glass is unique in many ash deposits. Also, most or all ash deposits from one volcano commonly have some chemical characteristics of their glass

Mount Iliamna, south of Mount Redoubt on the west side of Cook Inlet, occasionally vents steam, although the mountain has not erupted ash or magma recently. *(Steve McCutcheon)*

Because of its island setting, ash deposits from Augustine Volcano are more difficult to study. Preliminary results suggest that Augustine has been about as active as Redoubt during the past 10,000 years.

The largest ash deposit of the Cook Inlet region, however, was produced by a volcano that no one even knew existed until geologists traced its ash deposit in the direction in which it became thicker and coarser. Hayes Volcano is now but a few rocks sticking through Hayes Glacier in the Tordrillo Mountains 100 miles northwest of Anchorage. About 3,600 years ago, the volcano destroyed itself in seven violent eruptions that occurred during the course of about a century. *Each* eruption produced as much ash as did the May 18, 1980, eruption of Mount St. Helens. Hayes' ash deposit has been found as far south as Homer and as far northeast as Delta Junction; it was the heaviest ashfall in the past 10,000 years at Anchorage, where it can be recognized in most fresh excavations as pale pink and gray

that distinguish them from deposits of other volcanoes. Because glass is readily separated from the other materials composing ash and analyzed, it provides "fingerprints" by which distant ash deposits can be assigned to a source.

Geologists studying ash deposits around Cook Inlet have found that

Redoubt and Spurr volcanoes have been the most active; *each* has produced 30 or 40 different ash deposits in the past 10,000 years that were carried east toward Cook Inlet. Few ash deposits from Iliamna have been identified with certainty, suggesting that this volcano has been in a period of comparative repose.

layers a total of about three-fourths-inch thick just below the base of modern sod and roots.

The study of ash deposits in the Cook Inlet lowland is of more than academic interest. Hayes Volcano, for example, was discovered only from its distant ash deposit in the lowland. More importantly, ash deposits in a lake or bog are preserved in the muds and peat in the order in which they fell, and interbedded organic materials provide radiocarbon ages of the ash deposits. Copious quantities of ash and coarser fallout do occur on the flanks of volcanoes, but the material has been jumbled by sliding, avalanches, glaciers and annual freezing and thawing. Moreover, interbedded organic material is rare or absent from the harsh environment of a volcano. Thus there is limited opportunity to reconstruct the eruptive history of a volcano from study of its near deposits alone.

Lastly, from a human perspective, it is important to determine which volcanoes have produced large ash deposits that were carried far from their source, and when. Most of the historic eruptions of Augustine, Redoubt and Spurr have not left detectable ash deposits more than about 10 miles from the volcano, yet geologists know from news accounts that ash eruptions in 1953, 1965-66, 1976 and 1986 were a nuisance to people and a hindrance to aircraft much farther away. Clearly these prehistoric ash deposits are evidence of less frequent but larger ash eruptions than have typically occurred in the past 150 years. The volume of ash produced by Redoubt in its 1989-90 eruptions seems to be roughly equal to the average of the large prehistoric ash deposits, that is, the 1989-90 eruptions may be been typical of large Redoubt eruptions during the past 10,000 years. With careful monitoring of the volcano and tracking of each ash plume, the ash produced by these larger Redoubt eruptions — which occur on an average every 300 years — should require only occasional diversion of aircraft and airport closures of up to about a day. The 1953 eruption of Spurr was typical of its eruption style of the past few thousand years. The Hayes eruption 3,600 years ago is a good model for the largest probable, and most unlikely, eruption of a Cook Inlet volcano. Effects would be similar to those experienced in Washington state during the Mount St. Helens eruption. Aircraft may be excluded from the region during the actual eruption — one or two days — and airports along the path of the plume could be closed for up to several days until ash is cleared from the runways. Even such a "maximum likely" ashfall, however, need be no more than a temporary nuisance more than 30 miles from the volcano, provided precautions are taken: protect machinery, avoid prolonged or repeated exposure and inhalation, avoid flying into a visible ash plume at any distance from the volcano.

Sulfur deposits, such as these on Augustine Island, are associated with fumaroles in many volcanic areas. *(Chlaus Lotscher)*

Bogoslof Island

Editor's note: *The preferred spelling is Bogoslof. In early reports, however, it is spelled variously Bogoslov and Bogosloff; the latter spelling being an attempt to distinguish the new formation (1883) from the old (1796).*

Representatives of the Russian-American Co. watched with fascination from the craggy shore of

Two tufted puffins perch on a vegetated ledge overlooking the volcanic sands of Bogoslof Island, home to a colony of Steller sea lions. Bogoslof, and nearby Fire Island, were designated a national wildlife refuge in 1909; the group is now incorporated into the Aleutian Islands Unit of the Alaska Maritime National Wildlife Refuge. (G. Vernon Byrd, USFWS)

Umnak Island as a boiling disturbance a dozen miles north of them, in the previously unmarked Bering Sea, gained substance.

A marine volcano had thrust its head above the sea's surface, creating land where none had previously existed. The viewers immediately named the new creation Bogoslof, "theologian," because it was St. John's Day, an important May 18 festival on the Russian calendar for 1796.

Of the creation, a witness said:

"Large flames of such brilliancy that on our island, twelve miles distant, night was converted into day and an earthquake occurred with thundering noises, while rocks were occasionally thrown on the island from the new crater.

"After three days the earthquake ceased, the flames subsided, and the newly created island loomed up in the shape of a cone. About eight years elapsed before the island was sufficiently cooled to permit its examination. "

Bogoslof continued to have brief periods of activity, and in 1883 a companion volcano was born. Erosion, volcanic activity and earthquakes kept the visible portions of the new island/volcano in a constant state of change. In 1883 it was reported by a passing ship to be having an active eruption, "throwing out large masses of heated rocks and great volumes of smoke, steam and ashes, which came from the apex and from numerous fissures, of which some were below the surface of the sea."

The island, which was to be named the "Jack in the Box Volcano" by a popularized report of its activity in the *National Geographic* magazine, was visited by the revenue marine steamer *Corwin* in 1884. One of the vessel's officers, 2nd Lt. John C. Cantwell, later reported:

"Approaching the island from the northeast it has the appearance of being divided into two parts, the northern portion being in a state of eruption and the southern portion a much serrated rock rising almost perpendicularly from the sea, while between the two and nearer the northern part of the new Bogoslov a tower-like rock rises with a slight inclination towards the north to a height of eighty-six feet. At a distance it might be easily mistaken for a sail

upon the horizon; for this reason it is called Ship Rock or Sail Rock. A nearer approach discovers the fact that the two elevations are connected by a low, flat beach free from rocks and affording an excellent landing place for small boats. The *Corwin* steamed around the northern end of the island and close enough to obtain an accurate view of the volcano. The top was hidden by clouds of steam and smoke which issued not only from the crater but also poured forth with great violence from rents or areas in the sides of the cone. On the northeast side these apertures are particularly well defined. I counted fifteen steam jets forming a group situated on a horizontal line about two-thirds the distance from the base to the apex of the cone. This group was the more noticeable on account of the force with which the steam escaped as well as the marked regularity of the spaces separating the vents.

"When the center of the island bore northeast and distant three-quarters of a mile the *Corwin* was anchored in

thirteen fathoms water and a boat lowered in which we proceeded towards the shore, sounding in from ten to twelve fathoms until within one hundred and fifty feet of the beach, when the water gradually shoaled and we landed without difficulty, the wind being light from northeast and the sea smooth.

"The narrow isthmus connecting the old and new formations is composed of a mixture of fine black sand and small oolitic stone, the greatest quantity of sand being on a line dividing the island longitudinally into two parts. During our stay the water did not rise high enough to cover this beach, but pieces of driftwood, algae, etc., found on the highest parts fully show that at the times of highest tides or during severe storms the entire isthmus is submerged.

"The sides of the new Bogoslov rise with a gentle slope to the crater, and the ascent at first appearance is easy,

Perry Island, Bogosloff Group Rose in Bering Sea Spring 1906.

5718

but the thin layer of ash formed into a crust by the action of rain and moisture is not strong enough to sustain a man's weight. At every step my feet crushed through the outer covering and I sunk at first ankle-deep and later on knee-deep into a soft, almost impalpable dust which arose in clouds and nearly suffocated me. As the summit was reached the heat of the ashes became almost unbearable, and I was forced to continue the ascent by picking my way over rocks and bowlders [sic]

Capt. M.A. Healy commanded the *Corwin* during the 1884 Bogoslof studies. He later skippered the U.S. revenue cutter *Bear* during her historic arctic operations. *(Alaska Historical Library, reprinted from ALASKA GEOGRAPHIC®)*

whose surfaces being exposed to the air were cooler and afforded a more secure foothold.

"The temperature of the air at the base was 44° and at the highest point reached 60°. A thermometer buried in the sand at the foot of the cone registered 44°, half-way to the top, 191°, and in a crevice of the ramparts of the crater the mercury rapidly expanded and filled the tube, when the bulb burst, and shortly afterwards the solder used in attaching the suspension ring to the instrument was fused. We estimated the temperature at this point to be 500° Fahrenheit. The temperature of the water around the island was the same as that of the sea, as observed on board the *Corwin* at the time, 40°.

"On all sides of the cone there are perforations through which the steam escaped with more or less energy. I observed from some vents the steam was emitted at regular intervals, while from others it issued with no perceptible intermission. Around each

vent there was formed a thick deposit of sulphur, the vapor arising from which was suffocating and nauseating in the extreme.

"An examination of the interior of the crater was not satisfactory on account of the clouds of smoke and steam arising and obscuring the view. On the northwest side the surface of the cone is broken into a thousand irregularities by masses of volcanic and metamorphic rock. On all other sides, however, the accumulation of ash and dust has almost entirely covered the rocks and the sides appear more even and less precipitous.

"A curious fact to be noted in regard to this volcano is the entire absence, apparently, of lava and cinder. Nowhere could I find the slightest evidence of either of these characteristics of other volcanoes hitherto examined in the Aleutian Islands. Small quantities of rock-froth

consisting of unfused particles in a semi-fused mass were seen, but the heat of discharge has evidently never been sufficient to produce firm fusion. Specimens of dust collected from one of the vents was compared with volcanic dust which fell in the village of Ounalaska [Unalaska] October 20, 1883, and found to be identical in character.

"Descending to the beach on the east side I found it to be much the same formation as on the west side, with perhaps the exception that the line of sand here approaches nearer the water-line. The pebbles seen on the island are universally of a dark-gray color, with small black spots and worn surface by attrition.

"I saw no shells and but little sea-weed. Kelp in considerable quantities, however, was observed close inshore.

"A walk of a third of a mile brought me to old Bogoslov, where the beach abruptly terminates. The northern end of this rock rises almost perpendicularly to a distance of some 325 feet. Its face is deeply indented at the base, forming a cave-like recess which gives the rock the appearance of leaning toward the north.

"Probably nowhere can there be found a better example of the disintegration of stone into soil by the action of the atmosphere. The composition of the islet was originally of slate or shale. It is now breaking down on all sides and crumbling to dust. The central portion seemed to be composed of a more enduring substance, but a close examination was impossible on account of the loose, crumbling nature of the rock forming the sides and the precipitous ascent. I fired a rifle-shot into a flock of puffin, myriads of which were perched in the clefts and niches of the rock, and when they rose small pieces of stone were detached and in turn displaced larger pieces of stone until a perfect avalanche of stone came down the declivity, scoring great ruts in the hillside and tearing up great masses of stone, which were dashed to pieces on the shore below.

"Specimens of outer rock were found at the base of the old Bogoslov, on the southern side, which, being struck with a hammer, crumbled to dust, in some cases deeply tinted with

Evidence of its volcanic origin abounds on the west side of Bogoslof Island, looking south from Kenyon Dome. Castle Rock, a remnant of the 1796 eruption, pierces the horizon at right. *(G. Vernon Byrd, USFWS)*

red, showing the presence of iron.

"Hard bowlders [*sic*] of some hard, smooth stone fringe the bases of both the old and new Bogosloff, but a careful examination of the surrounding waters, both in small boats and on board the *Corwin,* failed to show any outlying dangers. A spot of sand and pebble formation extends from the southern end of old Bogoslov four-tenths of a mile in a southeasterly direction, and, like the isthmus connecting the two islands, is probably submerged at times of highest tides or during severe storms. The depth of the water around the island is shown upon the chart accompanying the report.

"Puffin in great numbers were seen on old Bogoslov, and it is probable they make this isolated spot a breeding place. I also saw numbers of harlequin-ducks, gulls, and kittiwakes. A dead albatross was picked up on the beach, but it is probable it was washed ashore, as its presence in these latitudes is not common. Several herds of sea-lions were found on the beaches and on the rocks of the island. They evinced no fear of our party until fired into, when they entered the water and followed us from point to point, evidently viewing our intrusion with the greatest curiosity and astonishment.

"Angular measurements were made on shore by Lieut. D. W. Hall to determine the heights of the peaks and the dimensions of the island, with the following results:

	Feet
Height of east pinnacle old Bogoslov	334
Height of center pinnacle old Bogoslov	289
Height of west pinnacle old Bogoslov	324
Breadth of base old Bogoslov	933
Height of Sail Rock	875
Width of isthmus (narrowest)	326
Length of southern spit	1,824
Extreme length of island	7,904

"General trend of island, SE. by E. and NW. by W.

"By observations of Lieut. J. W. Howison the position of Sail Rock was reckoned to be latitude 53°55'18" north and 168°00'21" west.

"In conclusion, I have to regret that this subject, so full of interest to science, could not have been more satisfactorily discussed, but the relation which old Bogoslov bears to the new formation, the existence or non-existence of a crater in the latter, and the geological problems arising open up a field of inquiry too vast for me to enter. It is with this knowledge that this report has been confined to statements of facts and description of phenomena which fell under my observation during a reconnaissance of the island, and if any of them should prove a help to any others in their investigations the most sanguine hopes of the writer will have been realized."

In a separate report, Surgeon H. W. Yemans, U.S. Marine-Hospital Service, also aboard the *Corwin*, said:

"The recently formed portion of Bogoslov Island, Bering Sea, lies in the latitude 53°55'18" north and longitude 168°00'21" west, and is of nearly circular shape, about one half mile in diameter and distinctly volcanic in its origin. It has, in previous descriptions, received the name of new Bogosloff in contradistinction to the more ancient portion of the island, the two having been thought by those who first saw them since the recent eruption to be separate islands.

"The exact date of the advent of the new portion above the sea-level is not definitely known. Natives who were in that neighborhood claim to have seen smoke issuing from old Bogoslov during and since the summer of 1882, but as they were at a considerable distance and no evidences were to be discovered about old Bogoslov of recent eruptions, it is fair to presume

that what was seen arose from the new portion, which possibly had not at that time made its appearance above water. Although known to be in superaqueous existence some ten months at the date of this writing it had received no closer examination than that possible from the deck of a vessel distant half a mile until the visit of the *Corwin*, M. A. Healy, commanding, May 21, 1884.

"The credit of the first discovery belongs, I believe, to Captain Anderson of the schooner *Matthew Turner*, who saw and sailed partly around the island September 27, 1883. He describes it at that time actively erupting large masses of heated rock and great volumes of smoke, steam, and ashes from the apex and numerous fissures on the sides and base; while at night bright reflections of interior fires were distinctly visible. A few days later Captain Hayne, of the schooner *Dora*, also saw it, but did not land. He gives a description similar to that of Captain Anderson of its appearance.

"No earthquake shocks or other unusual phenomena were noticed on the neighboring islands at the time of the supposed eruption, though the two volcanoes on Akoutan [Akutan] Island ceased to smoke at about that time and have shown no signs of activity since.

"October 20, 1883, a shower of volcanic ashes fell at Ounalaska [Unalaska] sixty miles to the eastward, although it is possible that this pumice dust came from Mount St. [*sic*] Augustine, a volcano then active some seven hundred miles northeast of that place.

"May 21, 1884, at 4 a.m., the new formation was seen from the deck of the *Corwin*, as a dull grey, irregularly shaped hill of about five hundred feet in height, from the sides and summit of which great volumes of steam were arising, obscuring the upper third, and becoming detached, floated off on the northwest wind, then blowing, as cumulous clouds. At a height of about two-thirds of the distance from the base there issued, on the north side, a series of large steam jets, which extended in a horizontal direction completely across the northwestern face of the hill, which at that part was considerably flattened laterally and quite steep, giving it a very striking resemblance to a smoking charcoal kiln.

"On nearer approach what at first sight appeared to be patches of vegetation became visible. A closer examination, however, revealed their true nature — collections of condensed sulphur which had accumulated around the orifices of what had once been active steam jets. These condensations were still going on, each vent, in fact, having its encircling collection of condensed sulphur of various hues and tints.

"Steaming to within one-fourth of a mile of the south side of the isthmus, which was first discovered to form a connecting link between the old and new portions of Bogoslov, thus making them one, so to speak, the *Corwin* was brought to an anchor in thirteen fathoms of water, and a landing by boats was immediately made. But little surf was breaking on the beach, which at that point was composed of fine gravel and sand, and landing thereon presented no difficulties.

"The low, narrow intermediate portion of the island termed in this report the isthmus, lying between and connecting the higher extremes, is readily seen to be of much greater age than the newly formed portion, and had evidently been, previous to the recent eruption, a partially submerged spit, making out in a northwesterly direction from old Bogoslov; but the same force which pushed up the new addition elevated it also, especially that portion, the extremity immediately beneath the northeastern half of the new formation. The extent of this elevation, judging from the

barnacles and water-marks on Ship and other rocks, being some twenty or more feet. It is the extremity of this spit which forms a considerable part of the foundation of this new portion.

"But few shells were found on the beach, and the only vegetation seen was a few patches of kelp and some specimens of Fucacine thrown upon the beach. Myriads of sea fowls occupied the clefts and crevices of the rocky heights of old Bogoslov and on the beach and rocks surrounding that end of the island. Large numbers of sea-lions, some of immense size, were seen, but took to the water on our approach. Both birds and animals seemed to avoid the newer portion, on which I saw no animal life whatever.

"The temperature of the water at the place of landing was the same as that more distant from the island, 42°; of the atmosphere, 44°; and a thermometer buried in the gravel of the beach above high-water mark registered 44°. Already had the odor of sulphurous oxide become distinctly perceptible, which near the summit and in the depressions rendered respiration decidedly difficult.

"Following the beach to the southward, in order to get as far to windward as possible, the ascent was begun. For the first one hundred

yards the route lay over a gentle slope composed of fragments of rock thickly covered with loose ashes, into which one sank knee-deep at every step; then, as the sides became steeper, over loosely-piled fragments of rock, following the ridge until about two-thirds of the distance had been accomplished, when we were confronted by an insurmountable wall of rock (aqueo-igneous conglomerate), which stopped further progress in that direction.

"The great fissure extends in a northeast and southwest direction through the upper third of the hill, dividing it into two unequal portions, the southeastern part being much the smaller and lower one. The smaller portion is about one-fifth of the mass and was 403 feet in height. Owing to its top being obscured the height of the larger summit could not be definitely ascertained, but it was probably about seventy-five feet higher than its neighbor, certainly not over five hundred feet in all, which height it had probably never exceeded by more than fifty feet. No satisfactory examination of the interior of the great fissure could be made, owing to the steam, fumes, and heat rendering entrance into it highly dangerous if not absolutely impossible.

"The immediate entrance only was

visible, the clouds of vapor which arose from and almost completely filled it hiding the interior from view. Vents more or less active were abundant; the temperature of the interior of one of the smaller ones was 196°; the thermometer, laid on the surface in a sheltered situation, registered 56°, while when held at the height of the head from the surface the mercury fell to 49°. Water thrown upon the rocks at the entrance of the great fissure was immediately vaporized with a hissing noise. It was observed there and elsewhere that the discharge from the vents was perfectly regular, unaccompanied by much, if any, noise, and the ear placed upon the surface and over the larger of the extinct vents could detect nothing more than a faint "purring" or hissing sound.

"Finding it impossible to make the wished-for examination of the great fissure or to reach the summit, we descended and made a half circuit of the base, where a re-ascent was attempted. Steep and inaccessible walls soon stopped our progress,

however, and only about the same elevation as on the opposite side was reached, and similar success attended our efforts to penetrate or even obtain a view of the interior. The heat of this side was much greater than that of the other, both of the surface and the discharges, it being hot enough in one of the crevices through which steam was escaping to quickly melt the solder fastenings of the thermometer and expanding the mercury sufficiently to burst the bulb, although the instrument was made to register 260°F.

"It is much to be regretted that a thorough examination of the interior of the great fissure was rendered impossible, as much desirable information could doubtless have been obtained, for at its bottom would, in my opinion, be found the perpendicular stratum forced up at the time of eruption, elevating the softer strata into the two flanking ridges which form the apices of the larger and smaller elevations surmounting the hill. A few fragments of granitoid rock picked from the debris indicate the probable character of this intermediate stratum, no outcroppings of which were, however, visible. The flanking portions, indeed, almost the entire visible part of the new formation, had evidently once formed the bottom perpendicular stratum, of which latter Ship Rock is possibly an extension or more probably a forerunner."

Since its 1796 birth, Bogoslof has at times appeared to have one, two, three and four major vents, or peaks. Its last major activity was reported in 1931 but, for the handful of residents on Umnak Island, it is still a restless and worrisome neighbor.

The eroded remnants of an ancient volcano are exposed at Kettle Cape on Umnak Island in the Aleutians. *(Dee Randolph)*

Aniakchak Caldera

By Thelma Trowbridge

In 1931 we were at Snag Point on Bristol Bay, more than 200 miles from Aniakchak Crater near Port Heiden. In the middle of the night of May 20 came the feared major eruption.

Dishes rattled and fell from their shelves in our cupboard; our percolator lid slid off the stove; the books in the schoolroom tumbled down

I had hung out a big washing the

Aniakchak, on the Alaska Peninsula and focus of Aniakchak National Monument and Preserve, was the site of three explosive eruptions in May 1931. The volcano has been dormant since that time. *(Keith Trexler, National Park Service, reprinted from* ALASKA GEOGRAPHIC®*)*

evening before. We awakened next morning to see those lines of clothes, snowy-white the night before, turned to a dull, leaden blue-gray. Roofs of neighboring houses were dull, ashen gray; the snow-covered ground was the same color.

Captain Halvorsen, superintendent of the Alaska Packers' cannery at Chignik, estimated that at least one pound of ashes an hour fell on every square foot of ground there. Even as far north as the Kuskokwim district more than 300 miles to the north, one-fourth inch of ash covered everything.

That particular time of year was reindeer fawning time, and back of the Nushagak on the tundra where the deer are born, the ashes fell so thick as to cover all moss. The adult deer moved in search of food and left

the fawns to die. The moss that these deer finally did find was so coated with ashes and grit as to grind their teeth to the gums. Dead geese, ducks, swans and other birds floated down the rivers of the Alaska Peninsula. The cause of their death was found to be the swallowing of ash.

A queer phenomenon of nature was brought about at that time by rapid condensation of the clouds. Rain formed and picked up bits of ash, and as these fell they picked up more and more ash, becoming as heavy as mud balls. It rained these mud wads for hours.

My washing that had hung on the line during the eruption literally fell to pieces after about two more washings, eaten by the acid content of the ash.

Okmok Caldera

By Al Keller

Editors note: *Okmok Caldera, on Umnak Island, is rated as one of the picture-perfect volcanic phenomena in the Aleutians. The giant "bowl" is nearly round and measures 7.4 miles in diameter.*

It has often been studied by earth scientists and, occasionally, by nonscientists who happened to be in the area. The following is a firsthand report, first printed in The ALASKA SPORTSMAN®, *August 1949, of a descent into the caldera by two soldiers. As often happens, these "explorers" misnamed the object of their quest; they*

A steam plume wafts from Okmok Caldera on Umnak Island. (Dee Randolph)

assumed they were assaulting Tulik — a volcano on the flank of Okmok that has not been active in geologically recent times. They actually descended into Okmok, the source of the volcanic activity, minor explosions, lava flows and smoke, reported near the end of their story.

If you asked the average soldier who "did time" in the Aleutians during World War II to tell you about those faraway islands, he would probably soon have you believing they were completely devoid of beauty. I certainly thought they were until one sunny day on Umnak Island when a friend undertook to prove to me that beauty is where you find it, and you cannot find it anywhere unless you look for it.

It was in June 1943, when Adolph Tryba invited me on a trip to Tulik Volcano to take pictures of the snow-capped cone and attempt a descent into the crater. The volcano was not active at the time. Adolph assured me that the drop into the crater would be child's play — just a Sunday stroll. Of course I learned that Adolph was a former steeplejack, so it probably was just child's play to him. Unfortunately I am the type who gets dizzy standing on an apple box.

We loaded my pickup truck with lengths of rope, pieces of steel rods and some food. The lengths of steel, Adolph said, were to be driven into the walls of cliffs we expected to encounter and used as footrests.

After an hour's drive through the warm sunshine we arrived at the base

Not since 1845 has the snow blanket of Isanotski Peaks on Unimak Island been disturbed by a volcanic eruption. *(John Bauman)*

of Tulik and found we could drive the truck clear up to the rim of the crater by utilizing the beds of volcanic ash, which virtually covered the mountainside to a depth of 10 to 20 feet. The ash provided a fairly firm base for the wheels, and we made good progress as long as we were careful not to spin the wheels.

Soon we were up above the low-hanging clouds that clung to the slope of the mountain, and the sun once more broke through and dried some of the dew from our clothes.

We parked the truck as near as possible to the edge of the crater and looked over the situation. Although cloud masses hemmed in the mountainsides, the crater itself was clear. We could see the entire bowl from rim to rim, and make out tiny blowholes on its floor. We saw what appeared to be tiny rolling mounds of dirt, some shooting forth steam, others giving off a sort of colored gas. It was like looking down into a Grand Canyon on a small scale.

Adolph pulled out his pocket scale and after a few moments of calculation informed me that the crater was close to 6 miles across. Later we found it to be 1,345 feet deep, straight down from the rim. The heat of the crater apparently dispelled the natural clouds, giving the effect of standing in a huge well and looking up to the high blue heavens. Although we were standing on snow, the floor of the crater looked as hot and arid as a desert, which we later found was exactly the way it was.

The first part of our descent was fairly easy. We scrambled down a strip of rotten shale on our hands and knees, until we reached the bottom and found a sheer cliff. Uncoiling the length of rope, Adolph secured it to a good-sized piece of rock, dropped the other end over the cliff, and began his descent into the "Devil's Brewpot." I followed him and, except for almost being buried by a slide of boulders I kicked loose on the way, we reached the floor of Tulik's crater without mishap.

The rolling mounds we had seen from the rim turned out to be small mountain ranges, each mound a perfect cone made of black volcanic ash. One thing that surprised me was the ice mountains we encountered at various points in the crater. How they were able to withstand the heat was a mystery to me until I discovered that the volcanic ash, which lay 6 inches or more deep, acted as insulation against the heat. How the ice got there in the first place, I have not yet discovered. Crossing these ice mountains was rather hazardous because of the many deep, snow-covered holes we almost stepped into. It grew so warm we stripped down to our undershirts. Almost like summer in Florida or California.

By noon we had fought our way over obstacle after obstacle and found we had crossed only about a third of the crater's floor. After lunch we started back toward the cliff we had only recently come down, because I certainly did not relish the idea of spending a night in this beautiful but eerie place.

We were about halfway back to the cliff when I stepped into a snow-covered depression and turned my ankle badly. A close examination of the injured part showed no break, and with Adolph's shoulder to lean upon I managed to get to the base of the cliff just as the sun was disappearing for the night.

Obviously it would have been foolhardy to try scaling that cliff in the dark, so we were doomed to spend the night in the crater after all.

The temperature remained constant even after the sun went down, so we did not have to worry about freezing to death. The fear of falling rocks and the need for drinking water made us leave the shelter of the overhanging cliff and move back toward the center of the crater. In retracing our steps I stumbled onto a small clear space between two ice hills, where a little white stream was seeping from the ground. The ground was warm, so here we decided to camp for the night.

After binding my swollen ankle, Adolph went in search of water. Alone, all sorts of thoughts ran through my mind. Suppose the volcano suddenly came to life again? What if Adolph ran into a pocket of poison gas? What if — a dozen other possibilities, equally unpleasant. As I lay there I thought of my nice warm hut down at the post, and cursed myself for ever climbing a mountain and dropping into a crater just to see the beauties of the Aleutian Islands. Seemed to me I could have gone all my life thinking they did not have any beauty.

At last Adolph returned with our canteens full of water, and we

Tulik Creek cuts through this gorge, exposing jointed lava flows from Okmok Volcano.
(Dee Randolph)

Douglas Harris, Larry Queen and Connie Modrow inspect a rhyolite dike near False Pass in the Aleutians. Dikes form when molten rock is squeezed into a fracture within the Earth's crust. This dike is enveloped by the black, volcanic glass, obsidian, which formed when this hot magma was quenched by the saturated sedimentary rocks into which it was intruded. *(Dee Randolph)*

arranged our sleeping places as best we could on the hard ground. We could feel the warmth of steam heat underneath. My ankle was throbbing painfully by now, but I finally dozed off into a fitful sleep full of dreams, none of them particularly cheerful.

I do not know how long we slept. A trembling of the earth woke me, and the whole crater was alight with a rosy glow. That was a horrible awakening! Right inside a volcano, and it was coming to life! There was a deep, rumbling sound, and a nearby cone was hissing. About that time another cone some distance away burst forth with a magnificent display of pyrotechnics.

"Let's get out of here!" yelled Adolph.

"And go where?"

"Anywhere but here!" he yelled above the noise of the cones.

Using Adolph's shoulder for my

support and favoring my sore ankle, we fought our way toward the cliff, our only exit from the inferno. By the time we reached the cliff the shaking had abated, but rocks were rolling down the steep incline to the bottom.

"No time to try climbing," Adolph said, eyeing the falling rock. "We'll just have to hold out right here for awhile. Maybe this shake is just a little routine one."

"Sure," I said, "just practice. Probably does it every time before it blows its top." Maybe an hour before, even, I added to myself. I'd have given anything to get out of there, anything at all, but we were stuck.

Together we huddled a short distance from the cliff and waited for daylight. A fine black ash began drifting down upon us, and as suddenly as it had begun, the shaking stopped. The rosy light faded away and the crater resounded with a deafening silence.

"Just as I thought," Adolph remarked with new aplomb. "Just a routine shake. Probably happens every once in a while. Just seemed big

to us because we were scared to death."

The night slowly turned into day, and we could make out the outlines of the cones and ice mountains once again. We moved up to the cliff and studied its face to see whether the shake had changed the path we had used coming down. It was as Adolph had feared. The rolling boulders had started some small slides, which in turn had carried away a portion of our path.

"Well, looks as though we'll have to find another way out," said Adolph, studying the face of the cliff.

"Do you have any suggestions?" I

asked irritably. By this time my stomach was aching almost as badly as my ankle, and I was just plain disgusted.

"I suggest you sit down and just be quiet for a while. I'm going to follow the rim around and look over that slope over there to the right," Adolph answered, pointing to a steep, snow-covered slope that pitched almost straight up from the floor of the crater to the under edge of the top rim. My heart sank. It was a good mile and half to the slope he was looking at, and I was already exhausted. To reach this new possibility of exit we would have to cross a series of ice mountains

Incandescence appears on the slopes of Mount Veniaminov during this 1983 eruption. *(U.S. Geological Survey)*

65

This volcanic plug testifies to the ancient volcanic history of the Aleutians and islands off the Pacific shore of the Alaska Peninsula. The plug is often the last part of a volcano to erode; this example, known as the "Gibraltar of the Aleutians," rises 1,000 feet from sea level on Ukolnoi Island, one of the Pavlov group. *(Douglas Harris)*

and also a piece of the lava bed crisscrossing the floor of the crater. That lava bed was composed of huge chunks of lava resembling slag from a steel furnace. We had discovered its abrasive qualities when I had practically worn out a pair of boots walking a short distance on it. Now we faced the prospect of fighting our way over it again.

I settled myself on a convenient rock and watched Adolph's slow journey over the ice hills toward what he hoped was a way out of this beautiful crater. As I sat there alone, with only my thoughts for company, I imagined what my appearance must be. A generous growth of beard. Dirt-encrusted hair. Clothes dirty and torn and a swollen ankle showing through a slit in my dilapidated boot. Ha, the intrepid explorer. Nature Boy! Lover of beauty and the great outdoors.

The sun began to beat down, and it grew hotter in the crater. The sips of water I took from my canteen did not help much. The water had a decided sulphur taste, and as I had already found out, it possessed remarkable laxative qualities which did not add to my comfort.

Adolph flashed into view from time to time as he reached the peak of a mound. He would wave his arm at me, then disappear down the far side. Finally I could see his tiny form as he started to climb up the new slope he had chosen. I could see him cutting steps in the ice. The crater was wrapped in dead silence, punctuated by the sound of Adolph's pick as he drove steel rods into the ice for footrests. We shouted back and forth, and the echoes bounced off the walls of the crater.

After an hour of agonized waiting my heart leaped into my throat. Adolph was preparing for the final and most dangerous part of his climb. With one hand he clung like a fly to the overhanging cliff, and somehow with the other he drove steel rods into the face of the cliff until the rods formed a sort of ladder. Slowly, hand over hand, he pulled himself up. At times he seemed to hang on nothing but space.

Fingers crossed, breathing prayers, I watched spellbound. No one will ever know the relief I felt when I finally saw him pull himself into a sitting position on top of the cliff. He had made it, safe and sound, performed a feat of climbing which I would not have dared for any amount of money.

Sitting on the crater rim, shaking his clenched fists above his head as a sign of victory, Adolph rested for a while. Finally he rose and started toward the truck, parked near the rim. I waited patiently, wondering what next. When he reached the truck I could hear the engine start, then saw the nose of the truck appear above the spot where we had started into the crater.

I got up and staggered drunkenly

over to the base of the cliff directly under the nose of the truck, and Adolph and I carried on a discussion of how the winch on the truck could be used to help me up the cliff.

"I'll let down all the line I have," Adolph shouted. "You crawl up the slope as far as you can. Try to reach the line, and maybe you can get enough slack to tie it around yourself. When you get it tied, I will use the winch to lift you past all the washed-out places."

The idea did not appeal to me, but neither did the idea of remaining any longer in the Devil's Brewpot. I agreed to try.

Adolph lowered the line to its full extent, and I started crawling up the slope. Half an hour later, exhausted, mouth agape and sucking for air, sweat-soaked, my blistered hands found the end of the rope. A wave of relief passed over me as I cradled that rope lovingly. I hope that never again will such a trivial thing as the end of a rope mean so much to me! With hasty, nervous fingers I secured the rope under my shoulders.

"All right," I shouted to Adolph.

"Okay. Just take it easy, and you'll be all right. Just keep climbing, and I'll take up the slack in the rope."

Slowly I climbed, carefully, hand over hand, knees pressing holes into the rock, fingers clawing into each handhold, sweat running off me by the bucketful. I could hear the grind of the winch gears, and it was sweet music. A wonderful invention, the winch!

Adolph kept up a running conversation with me to ease my nerves. I did not dare look up or down. The only thing I saw was the rock directly in front of my nose. I will never forget the sulfur smell of the earth I had my face pressed against. What little that remained of my clothes was scraped off on the way up, and my bare skin scraped and slammed against the rock wall.

Those last few agonizing yards were the worst. The rope was taut over the bulge of the crater rim, and I hung out in space. Adolph ran back and forth, watching the taut rope and adjusting the speed of the winch. All the while I hung there, not daring to look up or down, just seeing the cliff in front of my eyes. All this time I had to keep my body twisted to protect my sore ankle, which was by now as tender as a boil.

Each yard seemed like a mile. Finally I heard a jubilant shout from Adolph, and heard the winch gear speeding up. I found myself jerked over the rim, and lying, battered and bruised, on the top of Tulik Volcano once more.

"Well, that wasn't bad, was it!" said Adolph, with a grin a mile long

A catastrophic volcanic eruption sometime in the last 2 million years formed Emmons Caldera on the Alaska Peninsula. Perhaps the source of the Old Crow tephra that blankets interior Alaska and Yukon Territory, this eruption is thought to be among the largest caldera-forming eruptions in the Aleutian arc during the time period that geologists call the Quaternary, i.e. the last 2 million years. Historically, the Emmons area is one of the most continually active volcanic centers on the arc. (Douglas Harris)

Lava flows from Pavlov Volcano on the west side of Pavlov Bay on the Alaska Peninsula during this 1987 eruption. *(Betsy Yount, U.S. Geological Survey)*

cracking his sunburned face.

"Hell, no. Just a Sunday stroll."

I am afraid I may have sounded a little angry at this point in our adventure. I looked down at my body, scratched and scraped and practically naked, and wondered what had ever prompted me to leave the immense comfort and security of an Army post in a war zone to embark on such an adventure.

Adolph was not exactly a rose himself. Normally very thin, he now looked like a starved hound. His clothing was also more or less tattered, and his beard was equally as long and dirty as mine.

"We'd better go back to the post before they start sending a searching party out for us," I suggested.

"I don't know about you, but I'm for having a snack."

I had forgotten how hungry I was. Now my insides began to growl for want of food. We soon had the gas pot going and snow melted for coffee. The apple pie the cook had enclosed in our lunch box went down soon after the canned beans. Feeling almost 100 percent improved, we started back toward camp. Soon we were bowling along down the ash beds of the mountain slope to showers, food and beds.

Suddenly Adolph applied the brakes and we came to a stop along the edge of a deep ravine.

"What's the matter now?" I asked.

"I want to show you the most beautiful waterfall in the whole wide world," Adolph said, leaping blithely out of the truck.

"You know what you can do with your waterfall!" I said with finality. I guess that guy really loved the great outdoors, but I had had enough of the beauties of nature to last me for some time.

We finally rolled into camp late that afternoon, and found ourselves the center of considerable commotion. Some of our friends were about to start out looking for us, and we had to answer a lot of questions before we could clean up and eat. The doctor at the hospital took x-rays of my ankle and said it was just a bad sprain. No bones broken.

Adolph and several others made a return trip to the crater a couple of months later. I did not go along — and they did not have any particular excitement on the trip.

Now, whenever someone tells me to go to hell, I can always say, "Brother, I've been there already, and I'm back!"

Volcanoes are considerate, in a way. They always give some sort of warning — rumblings, puffs of steam and fire and ash— before they really go into action. Two years later Tulik Volcano finally put on the gigantic show it had been practicing for. On June 4, 1945, the volcano broke out with an angry roar, belching smoke and flame. Soldiers at the Umnak base watched the glowing sky apprehensively through the night, and next morning the Commanding Officer gave orders to evacuate.

Prindle Volcano

By Tom Bundtzen

Editor's note: *Tom Bundtzen is a geologist with the Alaska Division of Geological and Geophysical Surveys and a frequent contributor to* ALASKA GEOGRAPHIC®

Prindle Volcano is a small, inactive basalt cone located near the source of the Dennison Fork of the Fortymile River, about 50 miles northeast of Tok in the Yukon-Tanana Uplands.

The volcano was first described by well-known U.S. Geological Survey geologist L.M. Prindle in 1905, and later named for him subsequent to his death. The Prindle cone is about 3,000 to 3,500 feet in diameter and nearly 300 feet deep.

Prindle Volcano is a youthful Pleistocene land form that erupted alkaline basalt lavas onto the surface within the last 10,000 years. Besides its position in Alaska's Interior in contrast to the Aleutian arc or the Wrangell Mountains, Prindle's geological significance is that the basalt contains peridotite and granulite inclusions originating in the Earth's mantle and lower crust respectively. In other words, chunks of the mantle and lower crust from 80 to 120 miles down were piped to the surface in volcanic eruptions. Prindle is of obvious interest to those studying these deep portions of the Earth not normally exposed at the surface. Other localities of volcanic activity in Alaska with pieces of the mantle or lower crust exposed include cones in the Imuruk Basin of the Seward Peninsula, Nunivak Island and in western Alaska near Marshall.

TOP RIGHT: Prindle Volcano's basalt contains bits of peridotite and granulite, rocks associated with material originating deep within the Earth. *(Tom Bundtzen)*

RIGHT: Farid Kutyev (left) of the USSR Institute of Volcanology in Petropavlovsk, Kamchatka, and Robert B. Forbes, State Geologist (now retired) of the Division of Geological and Geophysical Surveys, examines peridotite inclusions (in green at tip of hammer) in alkaline basalt of Prindle Volcano. *(Tom Bundtzen)*

Mount Edgecumbe

Editor's note: *This material is reprinted in part from ALASKA® magazine, July 1974.*

Mount Edgecumbe, an inactive volcano 16 miles west of Sitka in southeastern Alaska, is part of a Pleistocene and Holocene volcanic field that covers about 104 square miles on the southern end of Kruzof Island. The field consists of gently dipping flows, composite cones and

Dormant Mount Edgecumbe crowns this view of the Sitka harbor. The volcano, on Kruzof Island west of Sitka, represents part of a Pleistocene and Holocene volcanic field that covers the southern end of the island.
(Harry M. Walker)

air-fall ash and lapilli. Augite basalt seems to be the most common rock type.

With the exception of Quaternary vents on Lisianski Inlet, Chichagof Island, there are no known Holocene volcanic areas within 148 miles of Edgecumbe. The scattered vents of interior British Columbia are 148 to 198 miles away; those of southern southeastern Alaska, a few of which could be Holocene, are also at least 198 miles away. The field is distant from those in the Aleutian Islands and the Wrangell Mountains.

The Edgecumbe volcanic field is closer to the continental margin, as defined by the 100-fathom contour, than are the volcanoes of the interior conterminous United States, Canada and Alaska, and is even closer than

most of the Aleutian volcanoes. As a result, the Mount Edgecumbe field provides an information link between the continental volcanoes and volcanic seamounts in the Gulf of Alaska.

Unsubstantiated, and probably inaccurate, accounts of volcanic activity in the area within historic time have been reported, but radiocarbon dates show that the most recent major eruptions were 9,000 years ago.

The mystery of the April 1, 1974, "eruption" of Mount Edgecumbe was partially cleared up when *ALASKA®* magazine received a series of photos which explained why the extinct volcano suddenly belched black smoke after being asleep for years.

FAR LEFT: Mount Edgecumbe has not erupted in recent times, but its location close to the edge of the continental shelf makes it an important link between continental volcanoes and volcanic seamounts offshore. *(Staff)*

LEFT: A helicopter heads for Edgecumbe with special supplies for an April Fools' stunt. *(Dirty Dozen, reprinted from* ALASKA GEOGRAPHIC®*)*

LOWER LEFT: Volcano investigators found this message stamped in the snow near burning tires. *(Dirty Dozen, reprinted from* ALASKA GEOGRAPHIC®*)*

Known only to themselves (and perhaps a few thousand Sitkans), a group called the "Dirty Dozen" admitted to having planned for three years to activate the volcano. The weather had failed to cooperate until 1974.

Unable to charter a Sitka-based helicopter, the Dirty Dozen hired a Petersburg chopper to haul 70 old tires to the cold cone of 3,201-foot Mount Edgecumbe. Dedicated to adding fun to Sitka's life, the volcano revivers knew they had succeeded when police and firemen received volcano-alert calls during the 20-minute smoke.

Those who investigated the cooked-up cataclysm found "APRIL FOOL" stamped in the snow beside the burning tires.

Volcanoes of Alaska

This list includes all the volcanoes of Alaska that have been active since 1700, and selected dormant volcanoes. Volcanoes are listed by location, moving from east to west. Please refer to map on page 7. Volcano heights are from Alaska Volcano Observatory. Many of the early reports of volcanic activity indicated steaming or "smoking" only, which may or may not be associated with an actual eruption. (Sources: University of Alaska Geophysical Institute and U.S. Geological Survey)

Name	Latitude	Longitude	Height in feet	Number of recorded eruptions since 1700	Type of eruption*	Date of last eruption
Edgecumbe	57°03'N	135°45'W	3,201	0		
Prindle	63°43'N	141°38'W	5,125	0		
Wrangell	62°00'N	144°01'W	14,163	0	S(A?)	
Spurr	61°18'N	152°15'W	11,070	1	A	1953
Redoubt	60°28'N	152°45'W	10,197	4	A,D	1990
Iliamna	60°02'N	153°06'W	10,016	0	S	Continuous
Augustine	59°23'N	153°26'W	4,128	7	A,D	1986
Douglas	58°51'N	153°32'W	7,000	0	S	
Fourpeaked Mountain	58°46'N	153°40'W	6,771	0		
Kaguyak	58°37'N	154°03'W	2,956	0		
Kukak	58°27'N	154°21'W	6,700	0	S	
Denison	58°25'N	154°27'W	7,606	0		
Katmai	58°16'N	154°59'W	6,715	1	L	1912
Griggs	58°21'N	155°05'W	7,600	0	S	
Novarupta	58°16'N	155°09'W	2,760	1	A,D	1912
Trident	54°14'N	155°07'W	6,115	3	L,D,A	1975
Mageik	58°11'N	155°14'W	7,103	0	S	Continuous
Martin	58°10'N	155°21'W	6,103	0	S	Continuous
Peulik	57°45'N	156°21'W	4,835	1	S,A	1812
Ukinrek Maars	57°50'N	156°30'W	299	1	A	1977
Chiginagak	57°08'N	157°00'W	6,800	2	A	1929
Aniakchak	56°53'N	158°10'W	4,450	1	A,D	1931

*Type of Eruption: A - ash; D - dome growth; L - lava; S - steam; US - unusual seismicity

Name	Latitude	Longitude	Height in feet	Number of recorded eruptions since 1700	Type of eruption*	Date of last eruption
Veniaminov	56°10'N	159°23'W	8,225	9	L,A	1984
Dana	55°38'N	161°13'W	4,442	0		
Pavlov	55°25'N	161°54'W	8,262	41	A	1987
Dutton	55°11'N	162°16'W	4,834	0	US	1988
Frosty Peak	55°04'N	162°49'W	6,600	0		
Roundtop Mountain	54°48'N	163°35'W	6,140	0		
Isanotski Peaks	54°45'N	163°44'W	8,025	4	A	1845
Shishaldin	54°45'N	163°58'W	9,372	27	A	1986-88
Fisher	54°39'N	164°26'W	3,593	1	A	1830
Westdahl	54°30'N	164°39'W	5,118	7	A	1979
Pogromni	54°34'N	164°41'W	6,568	4	L	1830
Akutan	54°08'N	165°58'W	4,275	31	A	1988
Makushin	53°53'N	166°56"W	6,680	13	A	1980
Bogoslof	53°56'N	168°02'W	331	8	L,D,A	1931
Okmok	53°24'N	168°10'W	3,519	15	L.A	1988
Vsevidov	53°08'N	168°42'W	7,050	5	S,L,A	1957
Kagamil	52°58'N	169°43'W	2,930	1	A?	1929
Carlisle	52°54'N	170°03'W	5,000	3	S,A	1987
Cleveland	52°49'N	169°57'W	5,675	10	L,A	1987
Yunaska	52°38'N	170°38'W	1,804	5	A	1937
Amutka	52°30'N	171°15'W	3,498	6	L,A	1987
Seguam	52°19'N	172°31'W	3,458	6	L,S	1977
Korovin	52°23'N	174°09'W	5,030	3	L,A	1987
Kasatochi	52°11'N	175°30'W	1,030	3	S,L	1828
Great Sitkin	52°05'N	176°08'W	5,710	8	D,A	1974
Moffett	51°56'N	176°44'W	3,924	0		
Kanaga	51°55'N	177°10'W	4,287	6	L	1933
Bobrof	51°54'N	177°26'W	2,421	0		
Tanaga	51°53'N	178°08'W	5,925	4	S,L	1914
Gareloi	51°47'N	178°48'W	5,160	10	A	1987
Cerberus	51°56'N	179°35'E	2,625	5	A,L?	1987
Little Sitkin	51°57'N	178°32'E	3,898	2	L,A	ca. 1900
Segula	52°01'N	178°08'E	3,786	?	A,L	
Kiska	52°06'N	177°36'E	4,004	7	L,A	1990
Buldir	52°21'N	175°55'E	2,152	0		

*Type of Eruption: A - ash; D - dome growth; L - lava; S - steam; US - unusual seismicity

Glossary of Volcanology Terms

By Dr. Juergen Kienle, Geophysical Institute, University of Alaska

andesite: a gray-colored volcanic rock that has a range of compositions, but is basically the mineral andesine (a feldspar) and one or more dark minerals, such as pyroxene, hornblende or biotite.

ash, volcanic: loose, aerially ejected material consisting of rock fragments and crystals under .08 inches in diameter.

basalt: a dark-colored volcanic rock composed of calcium-rich feldspar minerals and one or more dark minerals, such as pyroxene and olivine; it is lower in silica content than andesite and therefore less viscous as a lava.

bomb, breadcrust: the chilled crusts of breadcrust bombs are fractured by continued expansion of trapped gas within the still-plastic core.

bomb, volcanic: fragments of lava that are liquid or plastic when ejected, thus acquiring shapes, markings and internal structures from their flight through the air.

caldera: large, basin-shaped volcanic depression, more or less circular, the diameter of which is many times greater than that of the included volcanic vent or vents. There are two major types: (1) explosive, funnel-shaped calderas, (2) those formed by collapse along ring fractures.

cinder cone: the cone formed around the vent when the eruptions are exclusively explosive; the resulting cone consists of tuff and cinder.

cinder: small pieces of solidified, bubble-filled (vesicular), usually mafic lava from a volcano.

crater: (1) bowl-shaped topographic depression with steep slopes; (2) volcanic orifice.

earthquake, volcanic: seismic disturbances due to the direct action of a volcano or whose origins lie under or are closely associated with an active, dormant or extinct volcano.

eruption cloud: a rolling mass of partly condensed water vapor, dust and ash (generally highly charged with electricity), emitted from a volcano during an explosive eruption; may rise to heights up to about 30 miles above the volcano.

Continued expansion of trapped gas fractured the chilled crust of this breadcrust bomb on Augustine Island. *(Chlaus Lotscher)*

eruption, volcanic: ejection or emission of volcanic materials at the Earth's surface from a crater, pipe or fissure; their character varies from relatively quiet outpourings of fluid basaltic lava (e.g., Hawaii) to violent explosions accompanied by showers of volcanic ash typically from andesitic volcanoes (e.g., Aleutians).

explosion, phreatic: volcanic explosions, often of extreme violence, caused by conversion of water to steam.

fumarole: a hole or vent from which fumes or vapors issue; common in volcanic areas.

gases, volcanic: the primary magmatic gases emitted from lavas, either quietly or with explosive violence. Chief among these are H_2O, H_2, O_2, N_2, H_2S, SO_2, SO_3, CO_2, CO, HCl, Cl_2, CH_4, HF, Ar, He.

glass, volcanic: natural glass produced by the rapid cooling of molten lava.

glowing cloud (*nuee ardente*): very hot mass of gas and incandescent, fragmented lava. After ejection from a vent, usually horizontally, it behaves like an avalanche with extreme mobility.

hiatus: break or interruption in the geologic record or geologic processes.

lapilli: pyroclastics .08 inch to 2.5 inches in size.

lava dome: a plug or domical mass of viscous lava occupying a volcanic vent.

lava: the term includes both the fluid rock and the same material solidified by cooling.

magma chamber: a large reservoir in the Earth's crust occupied by a body of magma.

magma: liquid rock melt generated within the Earth.

mudflow: flowage of heterogeneous debris, lubricated with a large amount of water, usually following a former stream course.

neck, volcanic: solidified material filling a vent or pipe of a dead or extinct volcano.

Pele's hair: threads of volcanic glass (generally basaltic) drawn out from lava drops.

plug, volcanic: volcanic neck consisting of a single mass of solidified igneous rock.

pumice: excessively cellular glassy lava, generally composed of rhyolite.

pyroclastic: general term for fragmented volcanic materials of any size that have been explosively or aerially ejected from a volcanic vent.

rock, igneous: literally "born of fire," the name covers any rock formed by solidification from a molten state.

rocks, extrusive: formed by emission of molten rock magma at the Earth's surface.

rocks, intrusive: these arise when molten rock penetrates into or between other rocks, but solidifies before reaching the surface (c.f. extrusive rocks).

tuff: rock formed of compacted, small volcanic fragments smaller than .08 inches in diameter.

vent, volcanic: opening or channel in the Earth's crust out of which volcanic materials are erupted at the surface.

volcano: (1) vent from which molten lava, pyroclastic materials, volcanic gases, etc. come forth; (2) a mountain that has been built up by materials ejected from the Earth's interior through a vent.

Index

PHOTOGRAPHERS

ALASKA GEOGRAPHIC® back issues

Admiralty...Island in Contention, Vol. 1, No. 3. In-depth review of Southeast's Admiralty Island. 78 pages, $7.50.

Richard Harrington's Antarctic, Vol. 3, No. 3. Reviews Antarctica and islands of southern polar regions, territories of mystery and controversy. Fold-out map. 104 pages, $12.95.

The Silver Years of the Alaska Canned Salmon Industry: An Album of Historical Photos, Vol. 3, No. 4. Commemorates this historic era – late 1800s to 1970s – with text and more than 450 historic photos. 168 pages, $17.95. SPECIAL REPRINT!

Southeast: Alaska's Panhandle, Vol. 5, No. 2. Explores southeastern Alaska from Dixon Entrance to Icy Bay, including the Inside Passsage. Profiles every town, and reviews the region's history, economy, people, attractions and future. Fold-out map. 192 pages, $19.95.

Alaska Whales and Whaling, Vol. 5, No. 4. Examines whales in Alaska, with an authoritative history of commercial and subsistence whaling in the North. With fold-out poster of 14 major whale species in Alaska, color photos and illustrations and historical photos. 144 pages, $19.95.

Aurora Borealis: The Amazing Northern Lights, Vol. 6, No. 2. In this issue, Dr. S.-I. Akasofu of the University of Alaska, one of the world's leading experts on the aurora, explains in an easily understood manner what causes the aurora, how it works and how and why scientists are studying these amazing northern lights. 96 pages, $14.95.

Alaska's Native People, Vol. 6, No. 3. Examines the worlds of the Inupiat and Yupik Eskimo, Athabascan, Aleut, Tlingit, Haida and Tsimshian. Fold-out map of native villages and language areas. 304 pages, $24.95.

The Stikine River, Vol. 6, No. 4. River route to three Canadian gold strikes, the Stikine is the largest and most navigable of several rivers that flow from northwestern Canada through southeastern Alaska to the Pacific Ocean. Fold-out map. 96 pages, $12.95.

Alaska's Great Interior, Vol. 7, No. 1. West of the Alaska-Yukon Territory border, between the Alaska and Brooks ranges, lies Alaska's Interior. Includes an overview of this vast region, its rivers, communities and history. Fold-out map. 128 pages, $17.95. SPECIAL REPRINT!

A Photographic Geography of Alaska, Vol. 7, No. 2. A visual tour through the six regions of Alaska: Southeast, Southcentral/Gulf Coast, Alaska Peninsula and Aleutians, Bering Sea Coast, Arctic and Interior. 192 pages, $17.95.

The Aleutians, Vol. 7, No. 3. Reviews the chain of islands, home of the Aleut and abundant wildlife, site of a major World War II battleground and the heart of a thriving commercial fishing industry. Fold out map. 224 pages, $19.95. SPECIAL REPRINT!

Wrangell-Saint Elias, Vol. 8, No. 1. Alaska's only designated World Heritage Area, this mountain wilderness takes in the nation's largest national park in its sweep from the Copper River across the Wrangell Mountains to the southern tip of the Saint Elias Range near Yakutat. Fold-out map. 144 pages, $19.95.

Alaska Mammals, Vol. 8, No. 2. Reviews in amusing and exciting anecdotes and facts the entire spectrum of Alaska's wildlife, from immense polar bears to tiny voles. Includes each animal's description, range, life history, food and hunting/status. 184 pages, $15.95.

The Kotzebue Basin, Vol. 8, No. 3. Examines northwest Alaska's thriving trading area of Kotzebue Sound and the Kobuk and Noatak river basins. 184 pages, $15.95.

Alaska National Interest Lands, Vol. 8, No. 4. Reviews each of Alaska's national interest land (d-2 lands) selections, outlining location, size and access and briefly describes special attractions. 242 pages, $17.95.

Alaska's Glaciers, Vol. 9, No. 1. Examines in-depth the massive rivers of ice, their composition, exploration, present-day distribution and scientific significance. Illustrated with many contemporary color and historical black-and-white photos, the text includes separate discussions of more than a dozen glacial regions. 144 pages, $19.95.

Sitka and Its Ocean/Island World, Vol. 9, No. 2. From the elegant capitol of Russian America to a beautiful but modern port, Sitka has become a commercial and cultural center for southeastern Alaska. Author Pat Roppel, longtime resident of Southeast and expert on the region's history, examines in detail the past and present of Sitka, Baranof Island and neighboring Chichagof Island. 128 pages, $19.95.

Islands of the Seals: The Pribilofs, Vol. 9, No. 3. Great herds of northern fur seals and immense flocks of seabirds share their island homeland with Aleuts brought to this remote Bering Sea outpost by Russians. 128 pages, $12.95.

Alaska's Oil/Gas & Minerals Industry, Vol. 9, No. 4. Experts detail the geological processes and resulting mineral and fossil fuel resources that contribute substantially to Alaska's economy. 216 pages, $15.95.

Adventure Roads North: The Story of the Alaska Highway and Other Roads in *The MILEPOST*, Vol. 10, No. 1. This issue reviews the history of Alaska's roads and takes a mile-by-mile look at the country they cross. 224 pages, $17.95.

Anchorage and the Cook Inlet Basin, Vol. 10, No. 2. In-depth review of the commercial and urban center of the Last Frontier. With three fold-out maps. 168 pages, $17.95.

Alaska's Salmon Fisheries, Vol. 10, No. 3. This issue takes a comprehensive look at the past and present of Alaska's most valuable commercial fishery. 128 pages. $15.95.

Up the Koyukuk, Vol. 10, No. 4. Highlights the wildlife and traditional native lifestyle of this remote region of northcentral Alaska. 152 pages. $17.95.

Nome: City of the Golden Beaches, Vol. 11, No. 1. Reviews the colorful history of one of Alaska's most famous gold rush towns. 184 pages, $14.95.

Alaska's Farms and Gardens, Vol. 11, No. 2. An overview of the past, present and future of agriculture in Alaska, plus a wealth of information on growing your own fruits and vegetables in the North. 144 pages, $15.95.

Chilkat River Valley, Vol. 11, No. 3. Explores the mountain-rimmed valley at the head of the Inside Passage, its natural resources, and the residents who have settled there. 112 pages, $15.95.

Alaska Steam, Vol. 11, No. 4. Pictorial history of the pioneering Alaska Steamship Company. 160 pages. $14.95.

Northwest Territories, Vol. 12, No. 1. In-depth look at the magnificent wilderness of Canada's high Arctic. Fold-out map. 136 pages, $17.95.

Alaska's Forest Resources, Vol. 12, No. 2. Examines the botanical, recreational and economic value of Alaska's forests, and includes detailed information on the state's 33 native tree species. 200 pages, $16.95.

Alaska Native Arts and Crafts, Vol. 12, No. 3. In-depth review of the art and artifacts of Alaska's Native people. 215 pages, $17.95.

Our Arctic Year, Vol. 12, No. 4. This issue tells a compelling story of a year in the wilds of the Brooks Range. 150 pages, $15.95.

Where Mountains Meet the Sea: Alaska's Gulf Coast, Vol. 13, No. 1. Describes the 850-mile arc that crowns the Pacific Ocean from Kodiak to Cape Spencer at the entrance to southeastern Alaska's Inside Passage. 191 pages, $17.95.

Backcountry Alaska, Vol. 13, No. 2. A full-color look at the remote communities of Alaska. 224 pages, $17.95.

British Columbia's Coast/The Canadian Inside Passage, Vol. 13, No. 3. Reviews the coast west and north of the Coast Mountain divide from Vancouver and Victoria, including the Queen Charlotte islands. Fold-out map. 200 pages, $17.95.

Dogs of the North, Vol. 14, No. 1. This issue examines the development of northern breeds, evolution of the dogsled, uses of dogs and the history of sled-dog racing from the All-Alaska Sweepstakes of 1908 to the nationally televised Iditarod of today. 120 pages, $17.95.

Alaska's Seward Peninsula, Vol. 14, No. 3. This issue chronicles the blending of traditional Eskimo culture with the white man's persistent search for gold. Fold-out map. 112 pages, $15.95.

The Upper Yukon Basin, Vol. 14, No. 4. Monty Alford describes this remote region, source of one of the continent's mightiest rivers and gateway for some of Alaska's earliest pioneers. 117 pages, $17.95.

Glacier Bay: Icy Wilderness, Vol. 15, No. 1. Covers 5,000-square-mile Glacier Bay National Park and Preserve, including the natural and human history of the area, its wildlife, how to get there and more. 103 pages, $16.95.

Dawson City, Vol. 15, No. 2. Examines the geology and history of the Klondike, and why tourists want to go to Dawson while other northern gold-rush towns are only collapsed cabins and faded memories. 94 pages, index, $15.95.

Denali, Vol. 15, No. 3. An in-depth guide to Mt. McKinley, the Great One, and surrounding Denali National Park and Preserve. 94 pages, index, $16.95.

The Kuskokwim River, Vol. 15, No. 4. This issue focuses on the Kuskokwim drainage, from its source to the mouth on Kuskokwim Bay, including history along the river, mining, fishing, riverboats and village life. 94 pages, index, $17.95.

Katmai Country, Vol. 16, No. 1. This issue reviews the volcanic world of Katmai National Park and Preserve and adjoining Becharof National Wildlife Refuge. With fold-out map and index. 96 pages, $17.95.

North Slope Now, Vol. 16, No. 2. Much has changed since our original issue was prepared on the North Slope: the trans-Alaska pipeline, expanded oil development, new mineral finds, the debate over the Arctic National Wildlife Refuge. This issue brings readers up to date on the economic forces that have propelled the slope into the limelight. With fold-out map and index. 96 pages, $14.95.

The Tanana Basin, Vol. 16, No. 3. This issue acquaints readers with the contemporary lifestyle of the urban heart of interior Alaska and recounts her exciting history. With fold-out map and index. 96 pages, $17.95.

The Copper Trail, Vol. 16, No. 4. This issue reviews the Kennecott copper deposits, the Copper River & Northwestern Railway, Cordova and southeastern Prince William Sound as far east as the Bering River. With fold-out map and index. 80 pages, $17.95.

The Nushagak River, Vol. 17, No. 1. This issue reviews this important corridor for ancient men and early Westerners, and details the lifestyle and resources of one of the world's largest commercial fisheries. With fold-out map and index. 80 pages, $17.95.

Juneau, Vol. 17, No. 2. This issue takes an in-depth look at the state's frontier capital, a center of tourism, fishing and mining that has fought off attempts to move the seat of government and is currently seeing a resurgence in mining right at its back door. With index. 80 pages, $17.95.

The Middle Yukon River, Vol. 17, No. 3. Third in our in-depth series on Alaska's largest river. This issue covers the area from Fortymile near the Canadian border downriver to Holy Cross, where the interior gives way to the delta and the land of the Athabascan blends with that of the Eskimo. Fold-out map and index. 80 pages, $17.95.

The Lower Yukon River, Vol. 17, No. 4. Final segment in our four-part series on the Yukon River, this issue follows that mighty river from Holy Cross, through its broad delta to the mouth on the Bering Sea. The book includes details of history, communities, subsistence and arts and crafts of the region. With index. 80 pages, $17.95.

Alaska's Weather, Vol. 18, No. 1. This issue gives readers insights into the subject of the question Outsiders most often ask Alaskans: "What's the weather like?" In addition to a factual review of the state's weather, this issue provides glimpses into how Alaskans cope with their notorious climate. With index. 80 pages, $17.95.

NEXT ISSUE:

Admiralty Island, Vol. 18, No. 3. Home to a world-acclaimed wilderness and wildlife sanctuary, storehouse of significant mineral wealth and covered by thick forests of the Tongass, southeastern Alaska's Admiralty remains an island in contention. To members 1991, with index. $17.95.

ALL PRICES SUBJECT TO CHANGE.

Your $39 membership in The Alaska Geographic Society includes four subsequent issues of *ALASKA GEOGRAPHIC®*, the Society's official quarterly. Please add $4 for non-U.S. membership. Additional membership information is available on request.

Single copies of *ALASKA GEOGRAPHIC®* back issues are also available. When ordering back issues, please include a list of volumes desired and add $1.50 per book for 4th class postage and handling. To order memberships or back issues, please send your check or money order (in U.S. funds only) to:

The Alaska Geographic Society

P.O. Box 93370, Anchorage, Alaska 99509

The Alyeska Seafoods plant, part of Wards Cove Packing Co., lines the shore at Unalaska. The facility processes surimi; cod; fish meal and fish oil; king, red and *opilio* crab; salmon; halibut; herring and black cod. The parent company, Wards Cove, is owned in part by the Japanese firm Marubeni. (Harry M. Walker)

Japanese Investment in Alaska

By L.J. Campbell

In 1990, the Japanese for the first time surpassed the British as the leading foreign aquirors in the United States. This record-setting investment year for the Japanese — 179 deals worth $11.6 billion, according to the New York investment firm of Ulmer Brothers Inc. — culminates a five-year buying spree by the Japanese of U.S. securities, real estate and commercial concerns.

Japan's first investment in this country, however, was in Alaska, with a pulp mill in Sitka in 1953. Through the 1960s, Japanese capital investment in Alaska exceeded that of the other 49 states combined, and the pulp mill remained the largest single Japanese investment in the United States through 1973.

Long before Japan's recent emergence as a global economic power, Japanese capital and markets figured prominently in Alaska's economy. Alaska still has many of the raw materials Japan needs — timber, fish, minerals, oil, natural gas. Likewise, the Japanese have money to spend, consistently outbidding competitors for many of the raw resources. Alaska also has wilderness and wildlife, something the crowded island country of Japan lacks. This makes Alaska an attractive destination for affluent Japanese, some of whom have bought second homes here at comparative rock-bottom prices.

The relationship between Alaska and Japan has been cultivated by both sides. Alaska opened a trade office in Tokyo in 1965, the first state to open such an office in Japan; now some 30 other states have trade offices there. Likewise, Japan has had a Consulate General in Anchorage since 1971.

Without a doubt, Japan's interest in Alaska is far-reaching. Japanese companies have significant interests in Alaska's fishing industry. Japanese loans to shore-based processing plants are considerable, and some loans contain provisions to acquire a certain amount of the production as well as requiring employment of Japanese technicians. One out of every 16 fish processing plant employees are Japanese, working in Alaska on temporary visas and holding the industry's higher paying roe technician jobs, according to the state Department of Labor in March 1991.

Other significant investments by the Japanese in Alaska include Alyeska Resort, the state's largest ski resort for which owner Seibu Inc. plans a multimillion dollar expansion;

and development of a bituminous coal strip mine in the Matanuska Valley by an Alaska subsidiary of Idemitsu Kosan Co. Ltd.

Japan also is the state's largest customer. About 85 percent of the fish exported directly from Alaska during 1990 went to Japan, according to Bill Aberle with the Alaska Center for International Business. Japan buys 100 percent of the liquid natural gas produced by the Phillips Petroleum natural gas plant in Kenai. In 1990, Japan got about 70 percent of Alaska's direct timber exports, 56 percent of its petroleum products (mostly liquid natural gas and urea), and nearly 23 percent of its minerals. Of everything exported directly through the Alaska customs district in 1990, nearly 67 percent of it ended up in Japan.

Of course, Japan is not the only foreign investor in Alaska. The state attracts the fourth largest amount of foreign money of any state in the nation. Foreign investments of $17,982 million in 1988, the most recent direct foreign investment estimates from the U.S. Department of Commerce, put Alaska behind California, Texas and New York in value of direct foreign investments. The bulk of this — in dollars, number of firms and employees — comes from Canada, Japan, the United Kingdom and the Netherlands, although not necessarily in that order. The investments are not broken down by country when disclosure could breach confidentiality.

Of the total foreign direct investment in Alaska — $17,982 million — the value of Japanese investment was $36l million, the Netherlands' investment was $283 million; figures were not broken down for Canada, the United Kingdom or other countries. Through the late 1980s, Japanese affiliates employed

Japanese freighters anchor in Iliuliuk Bay, an arm of Unalaska Bay, to await a load of frozen fish for shipment to Japan. (Harry M. Walker)

the most workers of any foreign firms doing business in Alaska.

Here is a brief look at Japanese investments in the state by industry:

—FISHING—

The Japanese are by far the largest buyers of Alaska's fish, and have made substantial investments in fish processing plants here. These investments ensure that some fish will always be available for export to Japan.

Japanese companies control about a third of the state's seafood processing firms, according to the state Department of Commerce and Economic Development. Other foreign investors include Canadian, Korean and Norwegian firms. Japan is probably the single largest direct foreign investor in the industry, and is as large or

larger than all the others combined, says Paul Peyton, with fisheries development in the Department of Commerce and Economic Development, Juneau. Control can be manifested in ways other than ownership, such as buying contracts that determine a processors cash flow, he adds.

Depending on who is talking, Japanese investment in Alaska's fisheries can be seen as good or bad. But one thing is clear, says Peyton, "If the Japanese in the 1970s had not invested, a lot of companies would have gone down the tubes. The health of the seafood industry is in large part dependent on foreign capital."

Japan does essentially control the seafood market. The country buys about $12 billion worth of seafood a year, more than any other nation. It is an important market that Alaska's fishing industry is anxious to keep. Last year, Japan bought about $2 billion worth of U.S. seafood, most of which came from Alaska. Yet Alaska faces increasing competition in the Japanese market from other countries. The U.S. share of the salmon market in Japan has slipped from 85 percent to 70 percent in the past few years. Farm-raised fish shipped in fresh from European countries are cutting in on the popularity of Alaska's wild salmon, most of which arrives frozen in Japan. The Alaska Seafood Marketing Institute, the salmon industry's marketing arm, is spending $2.5 million this year to plug Alaska wild salmon in Japan.

Japan's interest in Alaska's fisheries goes back at least two decades. In the early 1970s, Japanese firms began investing in Alaska's fishing industry as part of their country's effort to diversify its seafood sources. Japan's prodigious seafood consumption sent its prodigious seafood consumption sent its fishing fleet all over the world. But as various countries sought to control the fisheries off their coasts, Japanese fleets found it difficult to expand or even maintain their high seas production.

In 1976, the United States extended its fisheries jurisdiction out to 200 miles with passage of the Magnuson Fishery Conservation and Management Act. This law effectively dislodged the Japanese-dominated foreign fishing fleet in the high seas off Alaska's coast, one of the world's most productive fishing areas. Japan depended on the Bering Sea and Gulf of Alaska for about 25 percent of its foreign catch. The Magnuson Act was phased in to "Americanize" the waters, allowing joint ventures between U.S. fishing boats and foreign-owned processor boats until 1991. Under the law, U.S. fishing boats must have at least 51 percent U.S. ownership, and the corporate board must have an American president and U.S. voting majority.

In the meantime, Japanese fishing and trading companies have continued investing in onshore processors, making some major new investments in groundfish processing plants in the last several years. Some of the major Japanese players include: Taiyo Fishery Co., Ltd., one of the largest fishing companies in the world that has been doing business here since 1963; Marubeni Corp., a trading company and one of the most active Japanese firms in Alaska's fishing industry; and Nippon Suisan Co., Ltd., one of Japan's largest fishing companies and a leading seafood-product manufacturer.

Various attempts have been made to determine the extent of foreign investment in Alaska's fish processing industry, but the exact dollar amount has been difficult to determine. Nine state agencies require information from companies intending to process seafood in the state, but much of the information is confidential or unreliable, in that it is not verified for accuracy.

A 1990 Alaska State Legislature study found: at least 23 percent of shore-based plants and offshore vessels had some foreign ownership; and more than 66 percent of the vessels listed in *Pacific Fishing* magazine's 1989 Factory Trawler Directory had at least partial foreign ownership. The study cited a

Filleted pollock is ground up to make surimi at Dutch Harbor for shipment to Japan. (Harry M. Walker)

1980 state report that said processers with partial Japanese ownership accounted for 33 percent of the total value of all species processed in state.

Yet the control and influence of foreign firms in the industry is likely to be much greater than the percentages indicate because of such things as pricing, marketing, loan agreements and the internal structure of the parent companies, the study concluded.

—TIMBER—

Alaska was home to the first Japanese investment in the nation, following World War II. The war had destroyed nearly half of Japan's forests, and lumber was needed for rebuilding. Representatives from Japan's timber industry approached U.S. authorities in Tokyo, asking to import timber from national forests in Alaska. In 1953, the Japanese-funded Alaska Lumber and Pulp Company was incorporated to operate a pulp mill in Sitka, and in return, the U.S. government guaranteed a long-term supply of timber from Tongass National Forest.

Alaska Pulp's capital was provided by Alaska Pulp Company of Tokyo, which authorized capital of $4,166,667 and paid-in capital of $1,041,667. About 60 percent of this initial capital was provided by 15 chemical fiber manufacturing companies (including all Japan's major rayon-producing companies), 21 percent by trading companies and 13 percent by pulp and paper companies. Later, the Alaskan subsidiary's capital was increased to $18.5 million through stock sales. In addition to the mill and 50-year timber contract, the company invested in a housing subsidiary, operated a store for its employees, and partially funded a dam and related facilities to provide water for the mill. Although it was granted a 10-year tax exemption in 1960 under the Alaska Industrial Incentive Act of 1957, it voluntarily began annual payments in 1962 to the city of Sitka to help cover school costs.

Through the 1960s and mid-70s, Japanese firms invested heavily in Alaska's timber industry, in sawmills, logging, processing and dock facilities. But by the beginning of the 1980s, Japanese corporations had all but pulled out of the timber business here for various legal and economic reasons. The Japanese housing market peaked in 1979; less timber was needed thereafter and the timber market declined.

The last big Japanese timber investment in Alaska to fold was a Tyonek wood chip mill owned by Mitsui and Company Ltd. The company in 1974 purchased beetle-infested timber from the state and planned to build a sawmill and chip mill to process it. Kodiak Lumber Mills (a wholly owned subsidiary of Mitsui U.S.A., which was a wholly owned subsidiary of Mitsui and Company Ltd., of Toyko) was formed to run the operation. But two things went wrong, recalls John Daly, an Anchorage-based consultant for Mitsui who was vice president of Kodiak Lumber at the time. The supply of timber, including the higher valued spruce, was half that projected by the state. The quality of the timber was also poorer. The sawmill never was built. The chip mill ran from about 1975 to 1982, but the company lost money and quit the business in February 1983.

Today, Alaska Pulp Co. is the sole Japanese timber interest in Alaska.

Japan remains, however, the biggest market for Alaska timber. Japanese buyers pay premium prices for Alaska's light-colored, tight-grained wood, a quality wood valued highly in Japanese culture and used for homes and furniture. The tight grain and relatively knot-free wood are characteristic of old growth timber like that from Alaska, and

Other bottomfish are separated from pollock on this conveyor belt at a surimi plant at Dutch Harbor. (Harry M. Walker)

worldwide supplies of old growth timber have been declining, says Eric Downey, timber market specialist with the Alaska Center for International Business.

In 1990, 70 percent of Alaska's direct timber exports were destined for Japan; more than 90 percent of the state's spruce logs and timber, sawn and rough-treated spruces, western hemlock lumber, and coniferous wood chips and particles went to Japan.

—TOURISM—

Japan plays a dual role in Alaska's tourism industry, as a direct investor and as a source for a potentially huge number of visitors.

An estimated 35 million Japanese, about a fourth of the country's population, can afford overseas travel and are among the highest per-day spenders, according to recent industry estimates. Japanese people, by all accounts, are fascinated with Alaska's wilderness, wildlife, and natural and man-made

spectacles, from the northern lights to the Iditarod Trail Sled Dog Race. Alaska is also considered a "safe" destination.

Of all the passenger traffic coming to Anchorage from Asia, 72.5 percent of it originates in Japan. Yet through the last decade, the number of Japanese visitors to Alaska has been only about 10,000 per year, compared with some 200,000 Japanese who visit Canada each year and 1.7 million Japanese travelers who vacation to Hawaii.

There are several reasons for the stagnation of Alaska's share; one of them is the problem Asian travelers face in getting here. Anchorage historically has been a stopover rather than a destination for Europe-bound international flights. Japanese tour wholesalers have had difficulty getting air seats confirmed from Toyko to Anchorage directly, and routing through Seattle is much more costly and time consuming, said Kojiro Abe, the state's tourism representative in Japan, in an *Alaska Business Monthly* interview. Also, aviation bilateral negotiations between countries affect airline routings and the number of landings allowed.

In the past two years, introduction of longer range aircraft that do not need to refuel in Anchorage and the opening of air space over the Soviet Union have translated to a steady decrease in the number of international passenger flights landing in Anchorage. Cargo flights are a different matter, as Anchorage is still used as a refueling stop. The designation of a foreign trade zone at the Anchorage International Airport helps make Anchorage particularly attractive as an air cargo hub, where shipments are transferred for worldwide distribution, particularly since Anchorage is equi-distant from the three major markets in the world, Asia, Europe and North America.

This drop in international passenger landings is expected to continue, as long as the major international airlines favor nonstop trans-Siberia and nonstop Asia-New York passenger routings. Six airlines that provided an Anchorage-Toyko link plan to reduce or suspend service through the next year, according to January 1991 data from the Anchorage International Airport. To counter this, Anchorage International Airport and the state are rushing to promote Anchorage as a passenger destination, hoping new air carriers will fill the looming void. A proposal is currently out to American Trans Air/All Nippon Airways to start an origin-destination route between Nagoya, Japan, and Anchorage.

Some industry observers say, however, that more investment is needed within the state — such as world-class resorts and accommodations — to cater to international tourists, particularly the upscale Japanese. Once the facilities are in place, the airlines will quickly follow, they say.

A Japanese company that has made a substantial investment in this regard is Seibu Alaska Inc. with its Alyeska Resort, a ski resort in Girdwood about 40 minutes south of Anchorage. Seibu purchased the resort 10 years ago from Alaska Airlines. The company's first major improvement was a detachable quad chair lift; the next was a lodge for day skiers. A hotel of several hundred rooms is planned in an upcoming expansion, to supplement the existing 29-room facility that now caters mostly to weekend skiers.

The expansion is estimated to cost $45 to $50 million. It includes the purchase and lease of about 100 additional acres for construction of the hotel, a new tramway and additional ski trails. The restaurant will be upgraded and an improved lift should almost double the number of skiers who can be accommodated, from 2,500 a day to 4,300 a day, according to the company's initial estimates. A major resort aimed primarily at Japanese visitors, and which would have been located north of Anchorage in the Talkeetna Mountains, was contemplated for a short time in the late 1980s by Mitsui and Company, Ltd. The idea fell through when Mitsui decided that the tourist market was not strong enough to make the resort profitable. Mitsui had acquired a development lease in a single bid for about 11,000 acres in the Hatcher Pass area in March 1987. The company proposed an aggressive development: ski runs from the top of Government Peak, a mountaintop restaurant, a ski lodge, condominiums, dude ranch and golf course. After surveying the market, Mitsui asked the state to extend the lease another five years or so while the market matured, during which time the company would continue payments. The state

The first Japanese investment in Alaska was the pulp mill at Sitka, which they have been operating since 1953. (Staff)

rerused and Mitsui withdrew without penalty in June 1989.

—REAL ESTATE—

Estimates of Japanese real estate holdings in Alaska are sketchy.

The U.S. Department of Commerce *Foreign Direct Investment in the United States*, 1988 estimates show Japanese firms with $49 million in commercial property in Alaska, out of the $252 million total commercial property holdings of all countries. British firms had $112 million in commercial property in Alaska, and those of the Netherlands had $53 million. No figure was given for Canadian companies, which is likely to be considerable. This figure includes gross value of all commercial buildings and associated land.

In what amounts to an interesting footnote, affluent Japanese citizens have bought a number of condominiums and single-family homes in Anchorage during the past couple of years. Stories about the depressed Alaska economy and surplus of low-priced homes appeared in Japanese publications and sparked the interest.

Erika Nishihara Boyd, president of Realty Center and one of the only Japanese-speaking brokers in Anchorage, has sold about 74 units to Japanese people since 1989, when she first begin getting inquiries. She has sold condos in the $30,000 range and single-family homes for as much as $300,000, doing about $3 million a year. Even the most expensive Anchorage homes are considered inexpensive by Japanese terms, she said. Many of the properties have been bought as vacation homes, close to wilderness and nature. An increasing number of Japanese buyers are showing interest in homes as investment properties that can be rented, Boyd said.

—MINERALS—

Japanese investment in mineral extraction has included coal research and exploration, long-term contracts for liquid natural gas, and some limited interest in oil exploration. It is expected that Japan will remain interested in Alaska as a source for raw minerals. The state has seemingly large amounts of increasingly scarce minerals, and there is some economic incentive offered by the short ocean shipping route. Production and development investment largely will depend upon world market conditions relative to Alaska.

A factor that undoubtedly has influenced the involvement of Japanese firms in oil exploration in Alaska has been the ban on foreign export of most of the oil produced here. Several laws pertain to this ban, which includes all oil except that produced on the west side of Cook Inlet. The bill that authorized construction of the trans-Alaska pipeline required North Slope oil be carried by domestic tankers and used in domestic refineries, with the exception of some oil destined for the Caribbean. The Export Administration Act, which is reauthorized periodically, is another law prohibiting export sale of Alaska's oil to foreign countries.

Through the early 1970s, Japanese firms had invested about $12 million in oil industry ventures, including $1.2 million in arctic slope exploration and geophysical surveys prior to the export ban.

Japanese companies may be more active in the oil-gas industry than public records show. Nippon Oil Co. has been involved in exploratory lease agreements on the North Slope for about the past five years. Even though a Japanese firm could not export oil from wells it might develop, the company could sell or exchange the oil for some that could be exported.

James Eason, director of the Division of Oil and Gas in the state Department of Natural

These logs are loaded at Hoonah onto a freighter bound for Japan. That country is the biggest market for Alaska timber, corralling 70 percent of the state's 1990 timber exports. (Harry M. Walker)

Resources says he is periodically visited by representatives from major Japanese trading companies. Japanese firms repeatedly express interest in buying the state's royalty oil from the west side of Cook Inlet, which amounts to about 3,500 barrels a day, but in three sales, the one-year contracts have always been won by Chinese Petroleum Corp., from Taiwan.

In the Cook Inlet and Kenai gas fields, Japanese investment is primarily in long-term contracts for liquefied natural gas (LNG) and urea. In 1967, Mitsubishi Gas Chemical Co., Inc., entered a joint venture with Unocal Chemicals to build a urea plant in Kenai, to use part of Unocal's natural gas supply. Mitsubishi owns 40 percent of the plant, and part of the urea is exported to Japan.

Since 1969, Japan has held a long-term contract for the total LNG produced in a joint venture between Phillips Petroleum and Marathon Oil Co. The Kenai LNG plant is operated by Phillips.

Japan's appetite for LNG is great; the country imports 70 percent of all the LNG traded in the world. Japan is targeted as a principal market by Yukon Pacific, the company that hopes to build a gas pipeline in Alaska for export of 14 million metric tons of LNG a year. So far, the only letter of intent issued to purchase gas has been from Korea for 2 million metric tons.

Mineral-related investments by the Japanese include:

• A major coal mine currently under development by Idemitsu Alaska Inc. in the Matanuska Valley.

Idemitsu has purchased a long-term state coal lease for the Wishbone Hill coal mine about 45 miles northeast of Anchorage, near Sutton. Idemitsu Alaska is a subsidiary of Idemitsu Kosan Co., Ltd., the largest independent oil company in Japan currently involved in coal development and mining activities worldwide.

Exploration and development of Wishbone Hill started in 1983. So far, Idemitsu has spent about $9 million on the project. The initial capital investment will be about $43.5 million. The state's permitting process for the strip mine is currently on hold, however, pending resolution of a land dispute. Production could start one to two years after the mine permit is issued, the company says.

Idemitsu Kosan plans to market the mine's bituminous coal to Japanese power utilities, shipping it to Japan from the coal loadout terminal at the Port of Seward. The coal will be trucked from Sutton down the Glenn Highway to Palmer, and shipped by train to Seward. The state has committed $9 million to buy a coal train for the Alaska Railroad. More than $10 million in highway improvements will be shared by the state, the federal government and Idemitsu. The mine will provide about 200 jobs at peak production with an annual payroll of about $11 million.

The company estimates the reserve at 14.5 million metric tons, enough to keep the mine going for about 16 years. The mine's coal will more than double the state's coal exports.

• Nippon Oil Co. investment in North Slope exploratory oil wells. On Jan. 29, 1991, Nippon North Slope Oil Co., Ltd. — in partnership with BP Exploration (Alaska) Inc., Texaco Producing Inc., and Union Oil Co. of California — won a state oil-gas lease in the Kuparuk uplands. The companies together bid on seven tracts, but were high bidder on only the one with a bid of about $36,000.

• A joint venture between Texaco Inc. and Nippon Oil Co. on the North Slope. This was an agreement for drilling exploratory wells in the Wolfbutton prospect, an area south of Kuparuk. Two wells were drilled in Wolfbutton, the last well drilled during the winter season of 1988-89, according to E.H. "Pete" Nelson, Texaco's Alaska land representative in Anchorage.

• Nippon Oil Co. also is a partner with BP and Texaco in another exploratory well drilled in the Wolfbutton prospect, the drilling completed in winter 1990-91.

• A 1981 investment in an unidentified Alaska coal mine by one of Japan's largest trading companies, Nissho Iwai Co., Ltd., was reported by the U.S. Department of Commerce, in its listing of foreign investments compiled from public sources. Nissho Iwai is one of the world's largest trading companies; a subsidiary, the Nissho Iwai American Corp., has an office in Anchorage. Nissho currently sells Japanese-made tubular drilling pipe to BP.

—CONCLUSION—

Alaska's abundance of natural resources, sparse population and lack of development capital has historically made the state an exporter of raw products, and Japan has been Alaska's largest buyer. Now state trade

The Japanese firm Seibu Alaska Inc. owns Alyeska Resort south of Anchorage in Girdwood. Largest downhill ski resort in the state, Alyeska plans a major expansion to improve accommodations, lifts and ski trails. (Harry M. Walker)

officials are interested in marketing processed and packaged Alaska products as well. Japan continues to be a principal market for these value-added products, with some success already for Alaska companies in selling berry products, vodka and glacier ice.

It is difficult to determine the actual extent of foreign investment in Alaska, including that of the Japanese; foreign companies often shield their investments in various ways. It is also difficult to say how foreign investments influence the structure, operation and politics of various industries. At the same time, it is clear that Alaska has courted foreign investments to help build the state's economy, and that the infusion of capital has brought jobs and diversified markets.

Investments in Alaska historically are seen as somewhat risky. That perception may largely be due to Alaska's historic role as a source and seller of natural resources.

"We're price-takers. We don't control the world supply in any commodity," explains Bill Paulick, with the Department of Commerce and Economic Development.

"That makes us somewhat risky. When you're only dealing in natural resource extraction, you're at the mercy of the world market. When worldwide demand is down, your investment is down."

The state is trying to change that, however, Paulick says. Telecommunications, higher technology and manufacture of value-added products are some of the areas the state is working in, exploring the possibilties project by project. While the bulk of Alaska's money probably will always come from natural resources, the state wants to see development of enough secondary processing to weather the down cycles.

STAN PRICE, BEAR MAN

He was known to visitors from around the world as the "Bear Man of Admiralty Island." For nearly 40 years, Stan Price lived among the giant brown bears of Pack Creek in Admiralty Island National Monument, carrying nothing more than a stout walking stick for protection.

In 1990, months after his death at age 90, the tidal flats where Price coexisted with bears were designated a state wildlife refuge in his honor.

The Stan Price Wildlife Sanctuary encompasses about 613 acres of state tidal flats, marshes and state waters at the mouth of Pack Creek. The creek flows eight miles east to Seymour Canal, at the mouth of Windfall Harbor on Admiralty Island's east side. The island is located midway between Juneau and Sitka in southeastern Alaska.

Admiralty Island teems with brown bears, about 1,500 of them, according to state biologists. With a bear per square mile, Admiralty has one of the densest concentration of these mammals in the world, rivaled only by Kodiak Island. Admiralty's bears and the island's dense nesting population of bald eagles led to dual designation in the late 1970s for much of its acreage as a national monument and national wilderness.

The Pack Creek flats have long been recognized as a prime spot to see bears emerge from the island's thick forests to feed on salmon. As early as 1934, Pack Creek became a bear sanctuary when some 5,000 acres of the creek's watershed were closed to hunting. The Civilian Conservation Corps even built a bear-viewing platform in a tree near the mouth of the creek.

Lt. Dr. J.P. Bell of Arkansas Center (left), Roy Cagle of Juneau and the late Stan Price share a snack at the Price homestead near Admiralty Island's Pack Creek. (Courtesy of Roy Cagle)

Stan Price came to live at Pack Creek sometime around 1952. In the years that followed, this colorful character would become as much of an attraction to visitors as the bears.

He was a thin, bespectacled man who wore a hearing aid in each ear and was seldom seen without his walking stick. He would smilingly greet visitors when they arrived at Pack Creek by boat or floatplane. They would often bring him food, particularly Neapolitan-flavored ice cream, his favorite. He would escort them on tours of "his" bears in the meadows and tidal flats. The bears were accustomed to him and paid little attention to his guests.

"He always said, 'Be nice to the bears and they'll be nice to you,'" recalls Price's nephew, Gary "Soapy" Lingle, of Juneau. Lingle visited his uncle often with deliveries of mail and fresh food.

Price lived in a house on a raft, a wanigan, and would often invite visitors inside to see homemade wildlife movies. He would send his guests home with raspberries, strawberries or whatever else was in season in one of his two gardens.

Price was born in Missouri and as a young man traveled through the western United States working as an electrical engineer. He got his first glimpse of Alaska during the early 1920s, when he served in the military. He returned to Alaska in 1926 in a homemade sailboat, drawn by the lure of gold. He spent the next 50-some years mining gold at Windham Bay south of Pack Creek, working as a logger, and running fox farms on three nearby islands. He visited Pack Creek several summers before he finally anchored his floating home here.

During that first winter at Pack Creek, he and his first wife, Edna, adopted an orphaned cub they called Belinda. This began a peaceful relationship with the Pack Creek bears, as Belinda returned with her cubs and they returned with theirs. As many as 25 bears would congregate here; the Prices had names for most of them. The bears would nose around Stan's woodsheds, clawing and biting his tools and rolling in the sawdust. They would occasionally wander into his garden, crawling under the three-strand electric fence he had erected to keep them out. It was not unusual, said his nephew, for Price to find a bear asleep in his woodshed in the mornings.

Price rarely clashed with the bears. Usually a loud admonishment or a spoon banging a pan would turn them away. He occasionally had to bonk one on its nose with his stick. "He said he hated to do that; they'd turn running, crying like a baby, and he knew it hurt them," Lingle recalls.

Only once, says Lingle, was his uncle injured in a bear encounter. Price and a strange bear surprised each other one morning on a path near his house. The bear stood up on its hind legs, swiped with its paw and knocked Price up against a tree, breaking his collarbone.

Word of Stan and the Pack Creek bears began to spread in the 1970s. They were featured on several national television programs, and Stan traveled Outside, to Nevada, California and Washington, to show his home movies as fund-raisers for various causes. The number of visitors increased. By 1987, nearly 1,000 people a year were visiting Pack Creek.

Wildlife managers worried that continued unrestricted access could lead to problems between the Pack Creek bears and people.

The thick forests of Admiralty Island shelter one of the densest councentrations of brown bears in the world. As early as 1934, Pack Creek, on the island's east side, became a bear sanctuary. (John Hyde)

The bears had lost their natural fear of humans. Some visitors, emboldened by the bears' apparent tameness around Price, were doing foolish things like walking between

sows and cubs, biologists said. Things worsened when a young sow named Pest started shaking down visitors for their lunches, charging at those carrying packs or bags.

Although rangers had been posted at Pack Creek since 1984, officials decided to take additional precautionary measures. In 1987, the U.S. Forest Service and the Alaska Department of Fish and Game decided to issue free permits and restrict people to the spit. The first permits were issued in 1988.

Also about that time, the biologists began spraying Pest with a cayenne mixture whenever she came within 15 feet of people. Normally, a problem bear like Pest would have been relocated or destroyed, but Price's friendship with the bears prompted other treatment. Repeated blasts of red pepper during the next couple of summers apparently worked. During summer 1990, Pest returned with cubs and behaved herself, according to monument officials.

Today, visitors are confined to a viewing area on the spit or to a newly built viewing tower upstream. Visitors are no longer allowed to wander the tidal flats or the meadows and must leave their lunches in a bear-safe cache.

In the last years of his life, Price made no secret of his disdain for the government's management policies, or the game officers' habit of carrying guns. Ken Mitchell, Juneau district ranger for the U.S. Forest Service, was Admiralty Monument manager when Price lived there. "Stan's view was that these people take their chances and if the bears eat them, then. . . His view of the world didn't take into account modern day liability," Mitchell says. "He was basically unhappy with the regulations."

Others were likewise unhappy with Price's unofficial homestead. They considered his collection of buildings an intrusion in the wilderness. The question of what to do with Price even became part of the public debate in federal planning for the island. The government decided to grant him a permit to live there.

Mitchell remembers trying to get Price to sign such a permit. "I'd go visit him. We'd have terrific discussions about the bears, the martens and mink around his place, the deer that came down in the winter that he fed. Then I'd say, 'Stan, we need to set up this permit,' and both of his hearing aids would fail simultaneously. End of conversation.

"To him, government was a bunch of incompetent bureaucrats who would mess things up, and he wasn't going to be a part of it. He basically lived there in trespass," says Mitchell.

"Stan was part of Pack Creek. He fit in. He understood the bears, the dog-eat-dog system of survival of the fittest."

During the last years of his life, Price spent only summers at Pack Creek; he could not do the work required to survive the winters. Sometime early in 1989, he started complaining of a sore on his neck which was eventually diagnosed as lymphoma, nephew Lingle said. Despite chemotherapy and radiation treatments, the cancer spread to his spine and paralyzed his legs. Price

died Dec. 5, 1989, at age 90, in the living room of Lingle's home in Juneau.

In June 1990, the Pack Creek tidelands were designated by the state legislature as the Stan Price Wildlife Sanctuary in honor of Price's unique relationship with

Stan Price first came to Pack Creek about 1952. After several summer visits, he anchored his floating wanigan here, and began the lifestyle that would eventually make him legendary as the "Bear Man." (Roy Cagle)

Admiralty Island's brown bears. At less than a square mile, it is the smallest state refuge.

The new designation gives state game officials the power to regulate visitation and activities on state property, below mean high tide in the boundaries of the sanctuary.

State wildlife managers say little will change in the operation of Pack Creek viewing areas for now. Free permits will continue to be issued on a daily basis. When the number of visitors exceeds 16 people on the viewing spit for five days a season, then a new system of issuing permits by lottery will start, said Dave Johnson, management coordinator for the Southeast region, Alaska Department of Fish and Game, Division of Wildlife Conservation.

In the meantime, government officials are trying to decide what to do with the legacy that Price left behind. His wanigan caved in last winter under the weight of snow, but his woodsheds and gardens remain along with stories of his pioneer spirit.

"How much should remain as a footprint that Stan was there?" asks Mitchell. "We have to get his friends, the environmental interests, together and decide how we're going to handle it. Is there going to be a visual reminder or will it be photographs in the Pack Creek brochure?"

For more information or permits, contact the U.S. Forest Service Information Center, Centennial Hall, 101 Egan Drive, Juneau, AK 99801, (907) 586-8751, or the Southeast Regional Office, Alaska Department of Fish and Game, P.O. Box 240020, Douglas, AK 99824-0020, (907) 465-4265.

Editor's note: *Look for in-depth coverage of Admiralty Island in a new issue of* ALASKA GEOGRAPHIC® *to be released in fall 1991.*

Environments NOW . . .

Scientists Solve Mystery of Duck Deaths

For the past decade, ducks and swans have been mysteriously dying in the Eagle River Flats north of Anchorage. Now, scientists with the U.S. Army say white phosphorus left over from munitions is killing the birds.

The Army has used the Eagle River Flats as a firing range for the last 50 years. Biologists first found dead birds along the edge of the 2,500-acre range in 1981. Since then, abnormally large numbers of swans and ducks — mostly mallards and teals but also some pintails, wigeons and shovelers — have died. While some estimates put the waterfowl deaths at between 1,000 and 2,000 a year, Army spokesman Chuck Canterbury said getting an accurate count is almost impossible.

"There are more dying there than should be," he said. "No other place in the country has this type of problem." Army researchers have called the mortality "catastrophic."

A federal-state-military team started investigating the Fort Richardson bird deaths several years ago. The Army spent $750,000 on extensive studies, which ruled out poisoning by heavy metal and polychlorinated biphenyls as well as being blown up or hammered by concussion. But investigators could not pinpoint the cause.

Then the Army's Cold Regions Research and Engineering Laboratory in New Hampshire went to work on the problem. After a nine-month, $305,000 study, the Army scientists in February 1991 identified white phosphorus as the primary culprit.

White phosphorus burns when exposed to air. Apparently as the birds feed, they ingest tiny bits of unburned phosphorus buried in mud. The birds become disoriented, stumble in circles and go into convulsions.

A team from the Army laboratory will spend summer trying to determine the extent of white phosphorus contamination in the flats. They will be looking to see whether it is widespread or concentrated in hot spots, and what can be done to keep it from killing more birds. Some possible methods of cleanup include removing or burying contaminated ground, or covering heavily contaminated spots with nets to keep birds from feeding in these spots.

Ridding the area of white phosphorus will not be easy. Artillery shells, rockets and grenades have been fired into the flats since the 1940s, but the number and type of munitions is largely unknown because firing range records were destroyed in a 1985 fire. Also, the area is littered with unexploded munitions, which makes field work dangerous.

The Army temporarily stopped using the wetlands as a firing range in February 1990. In September, Regional U.S. Fish and Wildlife Service Director Walter Stieglitz suggested the Army close the range for good and turn it into a wildlife conservation zone. It is considered by biologists to be the best wetlands habitat in the Cook Inlet area; between 3,000 and 5,000 birds flock to the range as a migratory staging area each year, said fish and wildlife service spokesman Bruce Batten.

The Army has no plans to permanently close the range, said Canterbury. It probably will be used on a limited basis this year as researchers study the problem. They also will try to develop a long-term plan so the firing range can be used with the least disturbance to the birds.

In any case, Canterbury said, white phosphorus munitions will no longer be used.

Northern pintails are just one of several waterfowl species affected by white phosphorus poisoning on the Eagle River Flats. (Penny Rennick)

On the Rim®...

Tim Viavant stocks arctic grayling fry into a pen. The fish are taken from a truck and loaded into an oxygenated tank in the boat for transport to the pens. Fish flow from the tank through this hose into the pens. (Tim McKinley)

Pen-raised Sport Fish A New Twist For Interior Lake

In an experiment in summer 1990 at Harding Lake, 44 miles south of Fairbanks, Alaska Department of Fish and Game (ADFG) Sport Fish Division staff successfully reared more than 300,000 rainbow trout, arctic grayling, arctic char and lake trout. The fish were raised in net pens for release into the lake's sport fishery stock. The biologists had tried rearing sockeye salmon in the same experiment, but were disappointed with the results when only 289 out of 100,000 sockeye survived. They had much better luck with the other species where mortality was minimal.

This is the first time in interior Alaska that sport fish have been reared in floating net pens in a lake. The project's purpose was to determine if sport fish could be raised in this fashion in a lake in the Interior. Biologists hypothesize that fish reared in net pens during the summer will contribute more to a lake fishery than fish released directly into a lake from a hatchery. The biggest potential benefit of the project would be creation of a major fishery close to Fairbanks.

(Excerpted in part from Alaska Sport Fish Currents.*)*

Scammon Bay Leather

Editor's note: *For more on Alaskins Leather, please see* The Newsletter *for* The Lower Yukon River *issue, Vol. 17, No. 4.*

Scammon Bay, a Yup'ik Eskimo village of 300 on the Bering Sea coast, has agreed to produce salmon leather items for Alaskins Leather Manufacturing Co. Recalling their tradition of making mukluks out of fish skins, Scammon Bay residents turned to Kuskokwim Planning and Management Corp. for help in working out an agreement with Alaskins. The Eskimos will purchase salmon leather and manufacture items, such as passport wallets, ladies purses and watch bands, ordered by the Juneau firm. The agreement will provide jobs for five Scammon Bay residents, will bring new dollars into the community and will provide villagers with regular hourly work where seasonal fishing has been the norm.

Coal River Hot Springs

Yukon Territory in September 1990 designated the Coal River Hot Springs as its first ecological reserve. The 3,900-plus acres of the reserve contain two hot springs bubbling out into turquoise-colored pools rimmed by terraced layers of the mineral travertine, or tufa. The terraced layers build up when the spring water at about 55 degrees dissolves calcium carbonate from under-lying rock and carries it to the surface. When the spring water touches the edges of the pools, the carbonate precipitates out and sticks to the rim, forming layers of the lightweight, spongelike mineral travertine. The process keeps repeating, causing the fluted edges of the pool to build higher and higher.

Layers of calcium carbonate precipitate from water at the Coal River Hot Springs in southeastern Yukon Territory. The hot springs area, about 48 miles east of Watson Lake, has become the territory's first ecological reserve. (Yukon Government)

— BIMA Leaves Nome —

The largest bucket line dredge in the world, the BIMA is nestled against a dock at Nome and surrounded by an ice berm during its over-wintering on Norton Sound. (Tom Bundtzen)

This closeup shows some of the new equipment developed by WestGold for mining offshore gravels. This submersible machine uses an experimental suction head to recover gold. (WestGold; courtesy of Tom Bundtzen)

Certainly the most famous floating dredge to sift Alaska's gravels in recent years has been the BIMA operating just offshore of Nome. 1990 was the dredge's last season. When a shaft on the bucket line broke, owner WestGold closed the operation and sent the BIMA south on a submersible barge.

Originally developed for offshore tin mining in the Far East, the BIMA came to Nome in 1986. Between 1986 and 1990, it produced 129,161 ounces of gold. In 1987 when its buckets scooped up 36,500 ounces of gold, the BIMA was the largest gold mine in Alaska. Other years it was second to the Valdez Creek Mine along the Denali Highway.

WestGold, North American subsidiary for Minorco of Luxemborg, a conglomerate with mining activities worldwide, knew by 1989 that the operation was not profitable. Several factors influenced their decision to pull out: The BIMA was not suitable for mining gold deposits in shallow water because it was bringing up too much barren ground in relation to the amount of gold; the operation was labor intensive, employing as many as 125 at one point; and operating costs were high for a five- or six-month season.

However, WestGold personnel did develop important technology and gain valuable experience during their years in Nome, including skill at using smaller submersible dredges. Some WestGold staff used a crawler tractor underwater with a suction dredge attached to the front to recover gold.

USSR Connection...

U.S.-Soviet Geologists Share Information

American and Soviet geologists are moving ahead on several fronts to share information on geological and mineral resources of Alaska and the Soviet Far East. A formal agreement, initiated in 1987 by the Far East Branch of the Soviet Academy of Sciences, has resulted in projects to exchange information and develop maps of mineralization on both sides of the Bering Sea. Spearheaded by the Academy and the U.S. Geological Survey, and later joined by the Alaska Division of Geological and Geophysical Surveys, the group has focused on publishing maps and articles on mineral deposits and tectonics.

Alaska has major lode deposts of copper-zinc-lead-silver sulfides, platinum and gold in its western region. But American geologists know little about the geology of their neighbor across the Bering Sea. Filling in the blanks in this knowledge could be important because the Bering Land Bridge, currently submerged, connects the two land masses. Since the U.S. claims jurisdiction of its continental shelf out to 200 miles, and since some mineral belts can extend for many miles, it is important for geologists on both

sides of the Bering Sea to be familiar with the geological history of the land bridge region.

The two-year programs spurred by the Academy in 1987 have already brought to light some information about mining activities in the Soviet Far East. According to an article in *Alaska's Mineral Industry 1989*, a state publication, the Magadan region produces about 2.5 million ounces of gold, 25 percent of the Soviet Union's total

production. Placer mines yield 90 percent of this total, 70 percent of which comes from open cut strip mines familar to many Alaskans. Dredges and drift mines produce the balance, and the Soviet Union had 247 dredges working its gravels in 1989.

A boron mine complex in the Primorye region north of Vladivostok is among the world's largest producers of this mineral used as a fixitive in production of glass, in manufacture of soaps and detergents, in production of agriculture fertilizer, insulation and in other industries. In addition, the Soviet Far East also has deposits of silver, tin, platinum, copper, lead and zinc.

In the private sector, an American group, Greatland Exploration, of Anchorage, has formed a joint venture with Bering Straits Trading Company and the Soviet group Severovostok Zoloto (Northeast Gold) to develop mineral deposits in both countries. Their first efforts focused on placer gold on Little Eldorado Creek north of Fairbanks and stone quarries in the Magadan region.

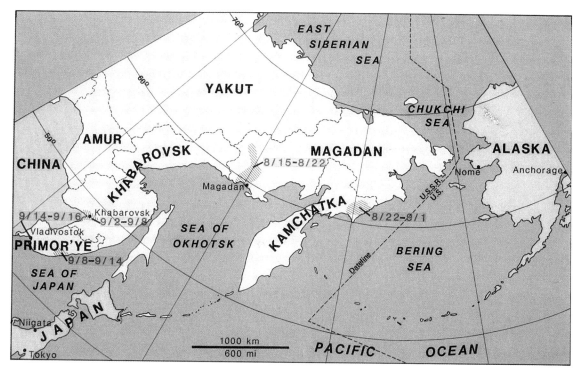

This map shows areas where American and Soviet scientists are conducting investigations of geological and mineral resources. (Courtesy of Tom Bundtzen)

Northern Ink . . .

THE GEOLOGY OF DENALI NATIONAL PARK, by Michael Collier, Alaska Natural History Association, Anchorage, 48 pages, 27 photos, 6 illustrations, 1 map, selected bibliography, no index, softcover, $7.95.

"Alaskan geology is still a wide-open game," says Michael Collier, author of this brief guide to Denali National Park's geology. After a short account of some of the region's early-day geologists, prospectors, miners and mountain climbers, the book discusses the various glaciations that scientists have identified in the Denali area.

"Geologist Clyde Wahrhaftig spent a good deal of time during the 1950s examining glacial terraces above the Nenana River. He sorted out evidence that suggested four major glacial pulses," writes Collier. Browne, Dry Creek, Healy and Riley Creek: the author dates each of the glaciations and describes their effect on Denali's geology.

Next comes an account of the rock types found in Denali — an account that in some cases could have used a glossary — and a time line for the region's geologic history. But what good is knowing the rock types unless the reader also knows what forces have made some rocks neighbors and split other rock communities apart. That is where the short chapters on structure and tectonics come in. "Structural geology is the study of rock behavior: given a particular stress, why does this rock bend and that rock break? The structural geology of Denali most basically concerns itself with three fundamental features: the Denali Fault system, the great thrust faults south of the

THE GEOLOGY OF DENALI NATIONAL PARK

TEXT & PHOTOGRAPHY BY MICHAEL COLLIER

Park, and the uplift of the Alaska range," explains the author. And basic to any understanding of faults and uplift is knowledge of the theory of plate tectonics, a theory of giant plates floating on the Earth's mantle and reshuffling the planet's land masses, threatening to carry Los Angeles north to Alaska millions of years from now. Collier gives a good account of tectonics in his final chapter, concluding "In simplest terms, Denali National Park can be thought of as three regions, each made up of a number of suspect terranes: land north of the Hines Creek Fault, land south of the McKinley Fault, and the land between these two faults."

But Collier readily admits that these theories are still evolving. "I'd sooner take my chances in a Fourth Street Saturday-night barroom brawl, than get caught between any two geologists trying to rationally discuss the ideas that have just been presented." Just so, but the foundations are there, in 48 pages of a classy, elegantly designed book on the story beneath the story of Alaska's "High One," Denali.

Order from Alaska Natural History Association, 605 West 4th, Suite 78, Anchorage, Alaska 99501.

–Penny Rennick

HOMESTEADING IN HOMER, by Elva Scott, R. Nelson Carnes and Associates, Pasadena, Calif., 1990, 48 pages, paper, $5.95.

This charming narrative of life in Homer, Alaska, comes from Elva Scott's diary, 1946-50. Scott's account brims with word snapshots of what it took to exist on the frontier, both in dollars and practical skills.

Her writing is breezy and down to earth; her insights wry and often amusing. About leaving for Alaska from California with her husband, Jim, their 3-year-old son and infant daughter, Scott writes: "Of course my Mother . . . was worried and cried the whole time, but then she always worried."

If Scott worried, she did not indulge herself on paper. She comes across as a hardy, confident woman who deftly mastered challenges of life on the edge. She tells about the growing community of Homer as well, get-togethers with neighbors, dances, fairs, ski club outings, the town's first telephone, the opening of the road to Seward.

Scott's publisher Nelson Carnes is also her nephew; as a 14-year-old, Carnes spent the

HOMESTEADING IN HOMER

BY ELVA SCOTT

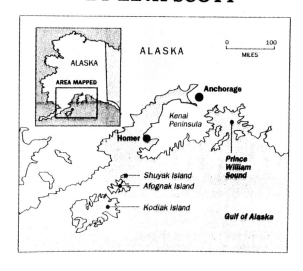

summer of 1947 with her in Homer. This pamphlet-style book sports a map on the front and contains more than a dozen black-and-white pictures. It is a quick, lively read; another sliver of Alaskana for the armchair homesteader.

Today, Elva and Jim Scott live in Eagle City, Alaska. She is retired from nursing; he is retired from the Bureau of Land Management.

Order from R. Nelson Carnes and Associates, 30 North Raymond, Pasadena CA 91103.

Published by
The Alaska Geographic Society

Robert A. Henning,
PRESIDENT
Penny Rennick,
EDITOR
Kathy Doogan,
ASSOCIATE EDITOR/PRODUCTION COORDINATOR
Kaci Cronkhite,
DIRECTOR OF SALES AND PROMOTION
Lori Granucci,
MEMBERSHIP/CIRCULATION ASSISTANT
L.J. Campbell,
STAFF WRITER

CALIFORNIANS ARRIVE

My Dad had decided to come up and help us with our building project. He built a two wheel trailer and packed in all of our items we had left in storage, mainly books. He pulled the trailer with a new Jeep, which he brought up for us. He was heavily loaded as he also brought Annie and our 15 year old nephew, Nelson Carnes. They were some of the first civilians allowed to drive on the Alaskan Highway. Annie only went as far as Anchorage. She had had enough and flew back to California.

ELVA DISPLAYING GRAYLING CAUGHT NEAR GLENNALLEN

The Fire Control Service folded the end of June as no money for the new fiscal year had been appropriated. We all returned to Homer June 28th with a new pup. Jim wanted to raise a dog team. Lots of work to do in the garden. Trying to separate the garden plants from the weeds and work on the cabin.

We spent another great 4th of July. Sixteen of our younger friends hiked in one mile to Diamond Creek with us. We fished for brook trout which were cooked and added to our picnic dinner. In the evening we all went to the show and dance.

OUR JEEP AND TRAILER BOGGED DOWN ON THE ALCAN